THE WARRIOR
Jeff Grayshon MBE

Maurice Bamford

Vertical Editions
www.verticaleditions.com

First published in the United Kingdom in 2011 by Vertical Editions, Unit 4a, Snaygill Industrial Estate, Skipton, North Yorkshire BD23 2QR

www.verticaleditions.com

ISBN 978–1–904091–48–6

A CIP catalogue record for this book is available from the British Library

Cover design by HBA, York

Printed and bound by Jellyfish Print Solutions, Hampshire

CONTENTS

ACKNOWLEDGEMENTS

I would like to thank Jeff and Sue Grayshon for their help putting this book together. Thanks too to Rugby League historian Robert Gate who with one of the game's top writers, Raymond Fletcher, formerly of the *Yorkshire Post*, helped me so much. Thanks also go to Roland Davies whose publication *Great Britain Rugby League Tours, 75 Years*, provided me with a wealth of information and to Graham Morris and Phil Hodgson whose books *Grand Final* and *Odsal Odysseys* helped with much of the finer detail, and to all Jeff's former team mates who helped me whilst preparing this biography.

INTRODUCTION

Birstall, geographically, is ideally situated in a fairly central position between the Heavy Woollen areas of Batley and Dewsbury, the mill town of Morley and the bigger urban sprawls of Bradford and Leeds. It is handy also for travelling to Halifax and Huddersfield and is only a stone's throw from the main motorways, the M62 and M1. It has an open market and has had connections in the past to the woollen trade, light engineering and the mining industry. One of its most famous sons was Joseph Priestley, the clergyman, chemist and one of the discoverers of oxygen. He was born at Fieldhead.

Birstall also has another famous son, it is the lifelong home of the subject of this book, the respected Jeff Grayshon MBE, a long serving and legendary international Rugby League forward. Apart from a spell when playing the 13 aside form of Rugby football in Australia for the Cronulla club, Jeff and his wife Sue have resided in Birstall for all their married life. He was born in the maternity wing of Batley hospital which is only a good punt of a rugby ball from Birstall town centre and his childhood began in Middlegate in the heart of Birstall. His career in Rugby League took him to five clubs as a player plus his stint in Australia saw him gain selection for Great Britain, England and Yorkshire and receive the prestigious MBE from Her Majesty the Queen at Buckingham Palace for services to his chosen sport. Jeff coached at two clubs and had his share of success in that field but it is for his long and devoted service as a player that he is remembered.

It was in 1968 that Jeff signed for Dewsbury after only a handful of games previously. Jeff was a 'late comer' to Rugby League as he'd been a better than average soccer player since being a boy at junior school. I first met Jeff in June 1972 when I joined the Dewsbury club as assistant coach. He was a quiet, unassuming young man who was an excellent tackler and a willing runner. Standing well over 6 feet and weighing, in those days, around 14 stone Jeff's amiable disposition made him popular with all at the club. In fact Jeff Grayshon was well liked and respected at all the clubs he represented. His easy going style comes through in this biography as we look back on a long, successful and distinguished career in the greatest game of all, Rugby League football.

1

EARLY DAYS

Jeff was born on 4 March 1949 at Batley Hospital. His dad, Jim Grayshon, was originally a miner at Shaw Cross pit and his mum, Mary Grayshon, worked as a weaver in the sheds. It was doing this noisy job that she learned how to lip-read, as most of the weaving lasses did. Later came along Jeff's two sisters, Rita and Susan. His early life was spent in the fairly rural surroundings of Middlegate with green fields around the working class houses. Jeff recalls, 'I hated school and even walking to school. The only day I enjoyed was sports day'. He began school at the Birstall Church School and later, at age 11, had to upgrade to the Batley High School with the rest of the 11 year olds. His sport in those days was soccer. Being a tall, well-built lad, the teachers saw Jeff as a natural centre half. His best mate and team mate at football was a lad named Stephen Butler who died tragically at age 15 of Leukaemia. Mr Butler, Stephen's dad, was an ex soldier and worked for years on the door of the Headingley pavilion in the Corps of Commissionaires and always made his way to speak with Jeff and Sue whenever Jeff was playing at the Leeds ground. One of Jeff's teachers, Mr Naylor, saw great potential in Jeff as a soccer player and looked after Jeff's advancement in the game advising him as to his strengths and weaknesses. Jeff was a key member of his side which won two Heavy Woollen schools cups in the same season.

Leaving school at age 15, Jeff landed a job in a Batley foundry as a moulder-caster. This was a noisy, dirty and dangerous job resulting in many burns and trapped fingers. Jeff batted it out for a month or two then managed to gain an interview for an apprenticeship as a pipe fitter-welder at Dawson's, another local engineering company.

Jeff still played football for Birstall Rovers in the Heavy Woollen league and such was his ability at age 15, he was invited to go along to Huddersfield Town at the Leeds Road ground, to train with them in the evenings and to have a few trial games with their junior side. Jeff went along with a mate from Birstall Rovers, played a few games and was asked to stay on but Town didn't want Jeff's mate and Jeff was having to pay his own expenses to get to and from training and matches. Not wanting to travel on his own he decided to say 'Thanks, but no thanks,' and went back to the Rovers.

It was whilst working at Dawson's that Jeff noticed a pretty young girl working in the office there. Her name was Susan and Jeff fell for her hook, line and sinker! They started going out together at the same time that Halifax Town contacted Jeff to ask if he was interested in playing a couple of trial games at The Shay. In those days, as today, one had to be outstanding amongst excellent players to sign as a professional soccer player, the best of the best. Halifax decided to let Jeff go and again he returned to the Rovers.

In January 1967, Sue and Jeff were married at the Wesleyan Chapel in Gomersal, Jeff was still only 17 years old. The pair set up home in a small back to back terrace house in Birstall and were happy from their first moment together. Jeff was working at his job as an apprentice pipe fitter-welder and was earning about £4 per week. Sue was now a housewife with a baby son, Paul. But on one occasion when Jeff's mum, Mary, called round to see Sue and Paul she was perturbed to see that there was not much food in the house. Sue explained to Mary that they did their shopping on Friday as Jeff was paid on Thursday.

Around this time, Dawsons entered a newly formed amateur Rugby League Sunday morning competition in the Dewsbury-Batley league designed to increase the amount of amateur players competing in the area. Jeff liked the look of this game and put his name down to play. Never having played competitive Rugby League before, he hadn't a clue where to play but the man in charge said, 'I want you to play full back' and gave Jeff a few tips on where to stand, how to tackle and which way to run when he received the ball!

Dawsons did well in this competition and Jeff's displays caught the eye of a Dewsbury club scout. 'Come training up at Crown Flatt next Tuesday Jeff,' he invited the tall, rather gangling six footer. Another young player had his first taste of Rugby League in this Dawsons team, playing either on the wing or in the centre. He too was spotted by the Dewsbury scout and made the transition to international and County second row forward for the Crown Flatt club. He also became Jeff's key partner in the highly successful Dewsbury side of the early 1970s. His name was John Bates. The committee let Jeff play three trial games and he began his Rugby League career as a full back for the Dewsbury 'A' team.

After Mary Grayshon had discovered the food situation at her son's home, she decided to do something about it. Telling Jeff's dad the story, Mary asked her husband to see if he could get Jeff a job with him. By now Jim Grayshon had left the Shaw

Cross pit and was working as a brick drawer at George Armitage's brick works in Leeds Road, Woodkirk. Jim managed to convince his employers to take on his son and consequently Jeff left his £4 a week job at Dawsons to become a £12 a week brick drawer at Armitage's. Jeff remained at this job for the remainder of his working life.

Jeff impressed the Dewsbury committee too in his three trial games and they offered Jeff the standard young player signing on fee of £100. Jeff signed and took the cheque home much to the delight of Sue who told me, 'We had never had a cheque for so much money before, it was a great feeling'. Jeff was now 19 years old and an impressive looking full back standing 6 foot 1 and weighing in at around 13 and a half stones. He picked up the correct attitude towards the game and as his confidence grew so did his reputation of being a veracious tackler and a strong running attacker. One tackle in particular stood out and caught the imagination of the committee and the club's coaching staff. In a game against Batley 'A', Batley's powerful prop broke clear and must have considered Jeff a soft touch. Running straight as an arrow at Jeff, the prop received the shock of his life when he was stopped with a crunching tackle, driven backwards and ended up in a heap, shaken and not feeling too well. It is said in Dewsbury club folklore that this tackle opened the first team door at Crown Flatt for Jeff and helped him put one foot firmly on the ladder to success.

Dewsbury Versus Oldham, (First Team Debut), Watersheddings, Oldham, 26 September 1970

When Jeff made his debut for the Dewsbury first team it was in the centre against Oldham at the Watersheddings. The result of the game was a close 17–16 win for Dewsbury. Scorers for

Dewsbury were Childe, Mick Stephenson and Nigel Stephenson (tries) with Nigel Stephenson kicking four goals.

Jeff recalls:

> With my previous experience in the 'A' team being at full back I found the pace much quicker in the centre in the first team. There was much more to do too and Nigel Stephenson kept me on my toes telling me to come across here, go across there, come nearer to me, go further away from me and so on. It was a real good experience and winning the game plus the winning money was excellent.

Jeff played in the centre for three consecutive games including Featherstone Rovers at home, won 40–0, Leigh at home, lost 16–3 and Keighley at Lawkholme Lane, lost 22–0. In the game against Leigh Jeff opened his try scoring account with a fine touchdown after a long run beating several opponents. It was a return to full back for the next game, a 20–17 win against Swinton, as he filled in for the injured Adrian Rushton. Jeff maintained his place in the first team when the recovered Rushton returned by reverting to centre for the next three games, a loss away to Barrow by 17–12, then a win against Doncaster and a try in the 25–2 victory and finally in this current first team run, against Rochdale Hornets at the Athletic Grounds—a 10–9 loss.

A run of eight first team games in a row was a tremendous help in building up Jeff's determination to return to first team duty. He said, 'I didn't realise that playing in the forwards would make such an impact on me. Looking back possibly Dewsbury may have made a slight mistake in continuing to play me in the backs. I don't mean anything detrimental against the club by saying that but my whole perception of the game changed when I did move into the pack'. Jeff's move to the forwards was still 10 months away and the thought of changing position from the backs into the pack was not an option at this time. This was because Jeff had begun his Rugby League life as a full back for Dawsons in the Sunday league only two seasons before and had only a handful of games in professional first team football.

So Jeff returned to the 'A' team and played five games there before being recalled to the first team where he appeared at full back in the first round of the Challenge Cup against the strong amateur side BOCM from Hull who had won through to the first round proper. The result was a 25–3 win, as expected, for Dewsbury. Jeff had played well in the 'A' team and thoroughly deserved his promotion as once again regular first team full back Adrian Rushton had received a knock which would keep him out for almost two months. Three further games at full back followed, Workington Town in a 7 points all draw at Crown Flatt, a 17–11 win over Doncaster at Tattersfield and a loss against Halifax at Thrum Hall by 15–9. Jeff was out for the following six weeks as an injury against Halifax at Thrum Hall laid him low. Rushton returned for two matches then broke down with a reoccurrence of his knee injury. Jeff returned to first team duty for the home game against Halifax which Dewsbury lost 22–10. That was Jeff's last game that season for the first team. Considering his late start and lack of experience as a Rugby League player, his 13 games in his first season in senior football was a job well done.

2

MOVING UP IN THE GAME

The Dewsbury side that was to become a force in the league had not yet developed. The team that reached the Challenge Cup semi final twice in two seasons and won so many friends through their style of rugby was still one season away. Jeff started this 1971–72 season playing 'A' team football. Adrian Rushton was fully fit again and playing well at full back. Nigel Stephenson was to play in every game this term as was Alan Bates at scrum half. Nigel's centre partners were, at various times, John Clark, Max Fletcher and Alan Childe. In the pack, Graham Bell, Jack Frain, Brian Taylor and Dick Lowe shared the prop positions whilst Mick Stephenson and occasionally his young understudy, Keith Voyce, played at hooker. The back three forwards alternated between John Bates, Glyn 'Harry' Beverley, Brian Robinson, Joe Whittington, John Clark and Kevin Osborne with John Bates being the leading second rower.

Jeff's form in the 'A' team was good and it earned him a substitute back's place in the visit to Blackpool Borough where Dewsbury fought hard for a 12–7 win. Joe Whittington had partnered John Bates in the second row that day but received a knock which laid him up for a couple of weeks. Out of the blue

Jeff was selected to take Joe's place and from that day on Jeff was a forward. He went in against one of the hardest packs in the game, St Helens, and played a blinder. Dewsbury lost 4–2 and Jeff's partner in the second row was John Bates. Jeff and John played many times together over the next few seasons, both becoming Lions tourists. Jeff remained a 'fixture' in Dewsbury's back row and became a superb international second rower and later prop forward commanding great respect.

My association with Jeff began in the season 1972–73 when I was appointed assistant coach to the head coach Tommy Smales. It was a wonderful season for the club with appearances in the final of the Yorkshire Cup, the semi final of the Challenge Cup and winning the Championship final. It was also, possibly more significantly, the season that saw the rise of the Dewsbury club from being a good middle of the table club to become a real challenger for honours in both the league and cup competitions. I also saw the development of Jeff Grayshon from a young, still inexperienced, forward into a full, almost classical second rower of international standard.

Jeff began to bulk up in physique becoming a big forward with pace. His ideal pairing with John Bates, another classical runner, gave the Dewsbury club a pair of second rowers equal to any in the league. The beauty of this pair of forwards was that not only were they quick and brave but also both were terrific tacklers. The partnership of Grayshon and Bates was the envy of most of the bigger clubs.

Jeff remembers one training evening vividly in the pre season. He had worked particularly hard that day in his job as a brick drawer. The work involved entering into the still-hot kilns and removing thousands of hot bricks to be stacked outside to cool and harden. There had been a rush on to get thousands of bricks out of the kiln and replace them, with still more bricks to be fired. It was back breaking work with little time for a rest and no doubt any lesser man would have taken an evening off from the punishing pre season work I was giving them. But not Jeff. Even though the fatigue from his strength sapping work told on him during the training session he never moaned, just attempted all that was put his way. I detected Jeff's running slowing, pulled him to one side and told him in no fancy way that this was not good enough. He returned to the squad, upped his efforts and was totally shot at the end of the session. Recently Jeff and I spoke about this incident and he explained the reason for his apparent lack of interest in his training. He said he was completely knackered from his hard slog all day at work. 'Why didn't you say something?' I asked.

Jeff gave that hearty laugh of his and told me, 'You wouldn't have believed me and I didn't want another one of your renowned bollockings!' He was, I suppose, a coach's dream to handle and possibly that was one of the reasons Jeff developed into such a great forward. He listened and tried his utmost to do what the coach asked. Jeff is a great guy and consequently became a 'father' figure to the youngsters coming through the club. He looked after them on and off the field with physical protection and sound advice.

Because of the great form of Jeff and John Bates, the coach, Tommy Smales, could concentrate on the problem position of loose forward. Brian Robinson was the most experienced man but Joe Whittington and Steve Hankins came into the equation too. Brian Robinson held the number 13 jersey almost throughout the previous season and Steve Hankins was a utility with the ability to play in the centre. The choice was Joe Whittington, who was slightly bigger and a stronger tackler than either Brian or Steve, and so played in the majority of games at loose forward.

The 1972–73 season began with a defeat at Clarence Street, York by 20–13 but four days later a fantastic 9–7 win at Central Park, Wigan against the mighty Cherry and Whites really set the benchmark for the remainder of the season where Greg Ashcroft scored Dewsbury's try and Nigel Stephenson kicked three goals.

A fine Yorkshire Cup victory of 19–5 over Castleford at Crown Flatt was followed by two further wins at home against Blackpool Borough 41–13 and York 29–16. Another County Cup win at McLaren Field by 20–8 put paid to the Villagers who had been a 'bogy' side for Dewsbury over the past few years. Then it was down to earth with a resounding 21–7 defeat at Naughton Park, Widnes against the Chemics. Barrow came from the North West to be beaten 22–11 at Crown Flatt, then came a nail biter of a Yorkshire Cup semi final at home against Halifax. Dewsbury went to the final on the back of a cracking 19–11 win over the Thrum Haller's. Wins against the amateur side Dewsbury Celtic in the John Player Trophy (22–4), a game that saw Nigel Stephenson receive an injury which would keep him out of action for 12 matches, and Whitehaven at the Recreation Ground (13–5) followed.

Dewsbury Versus Leeds, Odsal Stadium, Yorkshire Cup Final, 7 October 1972

Then came the chance to bring some silverware back to Crown Flatt when Dewsbury and Leeds met at Odsal Stadium in the Yorkshire Cup final. This was one game too far for the up and coming Dewsbury boys and Leeds dominated the play with awesome power and pace. The result was Leeds 36 Dewsbury 9. Greg Ashcroft scored the try and Alan Agar, on kicking duty for the injured Nigel Stephenson, landed three goals. Leeds scored tries through John Holmes (3), Les Dyl (2), Graham Eccles, Alan Hardisty and John Atkinson with Terry Clawson kicking five goals and Syd Hynes one. The Dewsbury team stayed at a Boroughbridge hotel the night before the game and arrived at Odsal in good spirits. The in-form Leeds had experience of how to win cups, which Dewsbury lacked. Dewsbury were to gain a great revenge on that same ground later in the season but for the moment they had to endure a hard learning curve.

The following four games were tough for Dewsbury as they fell within a 21 day period. They included Leigh away (lost 9–5), St Helens home (lost 17–12), Workington away (won 14–5) and St Helens away (lost 12–7). Again the scores show the toughness and closeness of all these games. Dewsbury had to regain their consistency as quickly as possible and another away game in Lancashire was not the easiest of passages. Blackpool Borough made the Crown Flatt outfit really struggle to gain a narrow 11–10 victory. The team's confidence had definitely dipped since the Leeds defeat and they needed a good set of wins to put them back on course.

Dewsbury's strengths were in their sound defence, a series of well drilled forward moves and the brilliance of the two players named Stephenson (Nigel and Mick). Nigel helped organise the backs from the centre position along with Alan Agar at stand off half. Nigel was also a first class goal kicker and his deadly boot won many a game for Dewsbury. The side missed Nigel's goal kicking and his marshalling of their attack. He had missed nine games through injury and whilst he was away for those nine games Dewsbury lost five. Another key player missing during this lean spell was top half back Alan Bates and whilst away Dewsbury lost five games.

The team tried various half back combinations as Alan Agar missed four games in the same period as Alan Bates and Nigel Stephenson. Steve Lee, John Russell and Steve Lane figured at number seven and Lane also moved into the number six jersey to cover for Alan Agar. The backs were sadly depleted, missing the three key play makers. But after being tumbled out of the John Player Trophy by Salford away and four losses in the league to Barrow away, Oldham home, Swinton away and Whitehaven home, results began to look up with the return to a full strength team.

Jeff had proved his durability by playing in every game for his club that season as Dewsbury set out on the Wembley trail with a tough first round tie at McLaren Field, Bramley. Reports on the game said that if Dewsbury went all the way to Wembley, this would prove to be their hardest earned victory. The score of 11–8 that gave the Crown Flatt men the win was not so much down to the try scoring ability of Mick Stephenson or Nigel Stephenson's accurate goal kicking with four out of four successes but more down to the dogged defence of Jeff along with prop Graham Bell. Jeff not only stood his corner in driving the ball in and supporting breaks by others, even making breaks himself, but also by the number of bone crunching head on tackles he made and his cover tackles on either of Bramley's wingmen were of a copy book nature for a second rower. The whole Dewsbury side responded to Jeff and Graham's defensive promptings and tackled their hearts out. The tigerish tackling by the Crown Flatt men and their fine defensive exhibition won the day. There followed two stiff away games at Rochdale Hornets Athletics Ground (won 20–6) and The Boulevard where the result was another fine 27–7 win against Hull FC. In the Challenge Cup second round Dewsbury's opponents were the tough tackling Workington

Town up at Derwent Park. Dewsbury had played Workington twice already in the league and knew what to expect up there in Cumbria. In the home league game Dewsbury held out against a fierce Town onslaught to win 11–6 and in the league game at Derwent Park, Dewsbury owed a lot to the grafting play of their pack in which Jeff and Joe Whittington were outstanding with a try apiece in the 14–5 win.

But Workington Town away in the Challenge Cup were a different proposition as the Cumbrians were fired up and the home side's feelings spread to the terraces where the fiercely partisan crowd were like an extra man to Town. It was as tough a match as anyone in the Dewsbury side had ever faced but with another almost superhuman effort and through tries by Mick Stephenson and Terry Day with two Nigel Stephenson goals, they came through victorious yet again with a breathless 10–8 win. In between the successful second round cup tie and round three was an awkward league game Huyton away. Alt Park could be a graveyard to good sides not taking the Liverpool outfit seriously. This point was driven home as Dewsbury had the following week's cup tie on their minds and were made to fight their way to a 9–7 win and they were at full strength to boot. Saturday 4 March 1973 drew a big crowd to Crown Flatt to see the crucial third round of the Challenge Cup against near geographical rivals Wakefield Trinity. This was a pulsating cup tie with play moving quickly from end to end of the field. Jeff had a hand in both the Dewsbury tries scored by Geoff Yoward and Nigel Stephenson: Nigel added four goals and Alan Agar one goal.

Around this time there was a strong team spirit in the Dewsbury camp. Great humour in the dressing room and a tremendous work ethic on the field yielded some terrific results. The good natured tricks included a send up of the two players who, when not playing, were almost always on the bench as substitutes, Steve Lee and Brian Robinson. They were ribbed regularly about their places on the bench and someone had made a visit to the train station where, in those days, one could print out one's name on a metal strip to be fastened to luggage. Whoever called into the station printed out 'Steve Lee' and 'Brian Robinson' on two metal strips and, come the next training evening at Crown Flatt, nailed them onto the back of the wooden benches in the dug out in the places where Steve and Brian sat! The place was in uproar with laughter when the strips were noticed and no one laughed more than Steve and Brian.

Although Jeff played in every game of the season and his partnership in the second row with John Bates was accepted as one of the best combinations in the game, his eye catching asset was his consistency. He was big, fast and strong and his stamina was honed on his job at work. His work rate never fluctuated, his tackling was deadly and sure, his covering work on defence was first class, as Jeff says with a wry smile, 'I once gave a start to Keith Fielding and caught him from the back!' Jeff will not elaborate on the situation that caused him to run down the very quick Salford pace man. Keith Fielding was regarded as the fastest wingman in the game at the time so the incident gives some indication of Jeff's speed. He was quick enough, on one occasion, to score a 50 yard try against one of the all round fast sides at that time, Hull Kingston Rovers. Some of his many line breaking runs against the top sides stemmed from his ability to move quickly for a big man. Dewsbury's work in this particular season had aroused the interest of not only the national pressmen but also the selectors of both the County and international sides. The work of several of the club's players had been seen, notably Alan and John

Bates plus Jeff. For pure consistency and enthusiasm these players stood out. It seems unfair to mention just three players who did so well as all the squad, under the excellent supervision of coach Tommy Smales, had welded into a hard to beat side who played constructive football with the added spice of forward set moves which opened the door in defences for the master skills of Mick and Nigel Stephenson.

So the Dewsbury team had reached the semi final of the Challenge Cup. The fixture set up meant Dewsbury had played only one of the other three semi finalists. The three teams besides Dewsbury were Castleford, Featherstone Rovers and Bradford Northern. Castleford had been beaten by 19–5 at Crown Flatt in the first round of the Yorkshire Cup in August 1972 but the Featherstone Rovers and Bradford Northern teams were both unknown quantities and the teams were 'on the up'. As far as Dewsbury were concerned, without being complacent, they had the beating of all four teams left in the competition. Dewsbury drew Bradford Northern in the semi final played at Headingley. If any team had the look of a Wembley finalist it was the Crown Flatt men. Playing with complete and utter confidence against all opposition, they were odds on certainties to march through to the then twin towers and cover themselves with glory.

But Bradford had other ideas and coached by the vastly experienced Albert Fearnley they had not had the best of seasons but were up for this semi final. Playing for Bradford was the streetwise middle back with years of successful experience for the Leeds club, Bernard Watson. Bernard was a local Dewsbury lad who knew the key men he was opposite and realised that if the Dewsbury backs worked off the foundation set by their excellent pack then Northern could be in trouble. He also knew the match winning qualities of Nigel

Stephenson.

Early in the game, Bernard caught Nigel with an absolute bell ringer of a tackle and the Dewsbury key play maker and goal kicker was in dream land for the remainder of the game. Albert Fearnley had also done his homework on the Dewsbury pack's style of play and the Northern forwards blocked every set piece and stopped Mick Stephenson's constructive dummy half play and his general support work which was so vital to the Dewsbury cause. The unstoppable machine that was Dewsbury's all season trademark ground to a halt and Bradford Northern's game exploded into action against a shell shocked and oh-so-confident pre match Dewsbury. The most surprised and heartbroken people were, in fact, the team who held a real dream of playing at Wembley but it was gone for another year.

There were six league games left after the Bradford Northern game, five at home at Crown Flatt. Dewsbury were handily placed in the league table for a tilt at the championship but obviously the favourites were the clubs in positions one and two in the league ladder as they had home fixtures in the play offs through to the final. The results after the cup semi final supported the Dewsbury team's determination to make up, as much as they could in the play offs, for the disappointment of the cup semi final. The games left to play were, Rochdale Hornets won 6–5, Warrington won 18–14, Salford won 14–7, Hull FC won 23–9 and Huddersfield won 18–8. The one away game was Huddersfield at Fartown, won by 22–14. So in that hectic rush at the season's end, Dewsbury won the last six games on the trot.

The good league results in the final games gave Dewsbury a home tie in the play offs against a strong Oldham outfit. Jeff scored a try in this game and had another outstanding run of form. Dewsbury saw off a strong challenge from Oldham to win by 29–14. Now into the last six sides still in the competition, the extra tough tie for them was against Featherstone Rovers at Post Office Road. Featherstone had beaten Castleford in the other Challenge Cup semi final and went on to beat Bradford Northern, Dewsbury's conquerors, at Wembley. But this was the quarter final of the Championship and Featherstone were one of the toughest teams to beat in any form of cup football. In one of their finest performances of the whole season, Dewsbury tore into Rovers hoping to knock them off their stride and also hoping that Featherstone had Wembley on their minds.

Dewsbury's 26–7 victory saw Mick Stephenson, Nigel Stephenson, Greg Ashcroft and Adrian Rushton scoring tries and Nigel Stephenson kicking seven goals. As usual I was sat on the bench for this game and remember distinctly Mick Stephenson's try. To describe this try may bring some doubt into the minds of students of the game but I can assure you it is an accurate description. Dewsbury were playing up the Featherstone slope and won a scrum five yards from their own line. Alan Bates at scrum half found Alan Agar with his pass and in turn Agar passed on to Nigel Stephenson who raced into a gap and went clear. Now all these sections of play went on continuously and as Nigel drew the full back onto him he passed the ball inside to the supporting player. That player was indeed Mick Stephenson who raced over under the posts.

I have often thought about the movement of that score. Remembering that scrums were highly competitive and that no doubt Mick Stephenson may well have, at some time during that scrum, been laid on the grass, he had to regain his feet and run 75 yards to accept Nigel's pass in the time it takes two passes and a clean break by a three quarter. I still cannot come to terms with the pace of Mick Stephenson's support run. It was an unusual and rarely seen try but never the less totally true.

Dewsbury played the Featherstone game on the Tuesday evening after their win against Oldham on the Sunday. The Championship semi final against Warrington at Wilderspool took place the following Sunday. This was the toughest, hardest game I can ever recall watching. Warrington had gained the services of arguably the best Rugby League player of his time, Alex Murphy. Alex, in turn, had signed the biggest, toughest pack he could muster with the classiest backs and was beginning to dominate both cup and league games. The game at Wilderspool was on a knife edge throughout and Dewsbury, again with outstanding performances from Jeff and John Bates who were subjected to tremendous defensive pressure with Warrington players frequently held on the Dewsbury try line. Surely the Yorkshire men couldn't hold out as time after time the big Warrington forwards smashed into the copybook tackles of Dewsbury's second row pair who stood their ground heroically. But hold out they did and with tries by Adrian Rushton and Nigel Stephenson and goals by Nigel, Alan Agar and Dick Lowe claimed a 12–7 victory in a game still remembered as one of the biggest upsets in many years.

As mentioned before, the Dewsbury side was packed with local talent and almost bursting to achieve something special. The side had international class players ready to show their potential on the bigger stage. The figurehead was the gifted hooker and captain, Mick Stephenson already an international and arguably the best all round hooker in the league as his play in the loose was superb either on attack or defence. Namesake Nigel was a points machine, a prolific try scorer, goal kicker and a maker of tries either at stand off half or in the centre. A pair of fast wingmen in Greg Ashcroft and Geoff Yoward, with Terry Day an excellent 'utility' back, John Clark, Alan Childe and Terry Day served up as first class partners for Nigel Stephenson to give Dewsbury some finishing power. The most underrated pair of half backs were in fact the exceptional Alan Bates and Alan Agar. Alan Bates did gain recognition with his selection for Great Britain and a place, with brother John, on the 1974 tour of Australia and New Zealand. Agar and Bates had a long spell of being the league's top half back club pairing. Alan Agar later continued a successful career, mainly at Hull Kingston Rovers and in coaching.

But it was the Dewsbury pack who shone week after week. Each man had a place in the various set moves suggested by coach Tommy Smales. The crowds were in awe at the sometimes complicated manoeuvres of the forwards as they set up from a tap penalty kick. In fact the moves were simple yet effective. The main ball carrying forwards at the completion of these moves were either Harry Beverley, Jeff or John Bates. The cornerstone of the pack was the experienced Dick Lowe. His handling skills and strong defensive input plus his great knowledge of the game helped formulate this highly mobile and positive thinking pack of forwards. The balance of the pack was completed by either Joe Whittington or Brian Robinson who both were accepted as the grafting tacklers. Jeff too was to become a terrific tackler either blocking the midfield or tearing across in cover tackling.

The scene was set then for a meeting, once again, with Leeds in the Championship final. The team did not want to face the disappointments of the Yorkshire Cup final in the defeat by Leeds or the total anguish of the loss to Bradford Northern in the Challenge Cup semi final. Coach Tommy Smales changed things around by not taking the players away before the game as he had done in the County Cup final.

Dewsbury Versus Leeds, Championship Final, Odsal Stadium, 19 May 1973

Tommy kept this final very low key in the dressing room and approached the game as if it were an ordinary league game. The 80 minutes of the game were viewed in a dream-like fashion. Time passed so quickly. Half time came and went and it seemed only minutes before the final whistle sounded. In between, of course, we had seen the talisman Mick Stephenson romp over for two masterful tries with the ever alert Alan Agar darting through for a special try and Mr Reliable, Nigel Stephenson, registering his now expected try plus landing five goals. The score of Dewsbury 22 Leeds 13 was no fluke. It was the product of a scintillating exhibition of speedy, high class and thoroughly entertaining Rugby League football in which Jeff played a major part. Jeff now had a major cup winners medal to go with his Yorkshire Cup runners up medal and the revenge for that County Cup defeat was now complete.

* * * * *

During the close season the Dewsbury players received a shock when the news broke that club captain and leader in chief, Mick Stephenson was released from Dewsbury to join Penrith in the Australian Sydney league. The move came out of the blue as two of the Penrith board arrived in Dewsbury and after a short discussion agreed a transfer fee. The two Australians came across to Harrogate where Mick was working for me as a plumber to interview him and away he went to seek his fortune in the land of sunshine. The damage done to the

Dewsbury side was immeasurable. Any club would have felt the loss of such a commanding figure but what made it worse for Dewsbury was that he was a local lad and adored by the club's spectators. Waiting in the wings was a young hooker who had understudied Mick for at least one season. So durable was Mick that young Keith Voyce hardly saw the first team. In fact his sum total of first team games in the Championship winning season was four. Into the deep end went young Voyce and he showed up well.

The season began with a 19–14 win at home to Featherstone Rovers. This was followed by a cracking 34–9 win at the Watersheddings, Oldham. Jeff was again outstanding in both opening games and indeed scored a fine individual try in the Oldham game. A trip to Belle Vue came next, two days after the Oldham match, and a rather unexpected 15–5 defeat at the hands of a keen and aggressive Wakefield Trinity side.

Five days after that the Yorkshire Cup began with a first round tie against Leeds at Headingley. The Leeds club must have rubbed their hands together at the thought of taking on Dewsbury again so soon after their defeat in the Championship final. In this game Dewsbury were never in the hunt and went down heavily 30–5. Jeff was by far Dewsbury's best forward according to the report in the *Yorkshire Evening Post* when it stated: 'Grayshon was all over the field tackling like a demon but even his great efforts could not stem the scoring tide of a determined Leeds attack.' Later the report said, 'Despite being beaten soundly Dewsbury's Jeff Grayshon never stopped running hard and was the only visiting forward to make any ground against this fierce home defence'.

Back on song the Sunday after, Dewsbury were too strong for a Whitehaven team and won the league game 22–10. When Jeff had settled into the first team two years earlier he had a pen portrait in the match day programme at one particular game. After the heading 'Ambitions in the game' Jeff had answered, 'To play at Wembley for Dewsbury and to play for Yorkshire County'. On 15th September he received a letter from Mr W.H. Hirst, the Secretary of the Yorkshire County Rugby League advising him that he had been selected to play for Yorkshire against Lancashire at Naughton Park, Widnes, on 19th September. A letter from the Chairman of the Yorkshire committee, Mr Doug Alton of the Bramley club, arrived on the same day congratulating Jeff on his well earned selection. So one aspect of his ambitions had been realised. At that time playing one game for the County earned you a County badge for a blazer, a beautiful White Rose. A second appearance earned you a County Cap which was a great achievement for any player. But Dewsbury had a key game before the County match that was against Widnes at Crown Flatt in the first round of the John Player Trophy. This was won 33–24.

Jeff's debut for Yorkshire County was an important game in as much as it was a play off for the County Championship. Both Counties had beaten Cumbria and a win was imperative. Yorkshire had made two changes to the side that beat Cumbria, Syd Hynes [Leeds] and Jeff replaced Les Dyl [Leeds] and Bob Irving [Wigan]. Winning the prestigious County Championship also brought with it the most beautiful gold medal, possibly the most ornate winners medal in the whole of the Rugby League's collection of superb medals. This was a typical inter County clash with tough tackling and thorough determination to win throughout the game. Jeff made a telling debut, demonstrating good form from the kick off. The pairing of Jeff and Jimmy Thompson in the second row was an instant success as both were excellent tacklers and willing runners.

Yorkshire Versus Lancashire,
Naughton Park, Widnes, 19 September 1973

The selection of John Bates as substitute forward showed just how much was thought of the club partnership at Dewsbury. The game was very closely contested and reports in the national newspapers said that the result could have gone either way. As it was both teams scored three tries, Billy Benyon, George Nicholls and Eric Prescott for Lancashire and Alan Smith, John Atkinson and Frank Davies for Yorkshire. Each side kicked three goals, Derek Whitehead for the Red Rose and Brian Jefferson for the White Rose. Lancashire won the game 17–15, the deciding drop goal coming from Leigh's Jim Fiddler. Reports echoed the fact that Thompson and Grayshon were outstanding in the Yorkshire second row.

All in all, despite the result, Jeff was satisfied with his debut and after tasting representative football wanted more. Some leading journalists were already bandying his name around for Great Britain or England selection and Jeff knew that consistent County selection could well open the door to international football. The inter County season had ended with the game against Lancashire and it would be next season before County selection would be possible again. This was totally dependent upon how well he was playing for Dewsbury and how well the County selectors thought he had done in his debut match. Another yardstick by which Jeff would be measured would be his form against the touring Australians in the winter of 1973. Jeff would have a chance to show his wares at this level when Dewsbury hosted the tourists on 7th October when they appeared at Crown Flatt.

Returning to club action against Leigh at Hilton Park, Jeff

had a new second row partner in Steve Hankins the excellent utility player. This was because John Bates had received a knock coming on as substitute in the County game and was unfit for the match at Leigh. Once again the Dewsbury side, led by a masterful display from their forwards, grabbed the spoils inflicting an 18–17 defeat in a memorable away win in Lancashire. St Helens proved too much for Dewsbury at Crown Flatt giving the home side a lesson in basic handling and support play. Saints won the game 21–8. Like almost every club in the league Dewsbury hit a spell when key players were injured. At various times they were without Nigel Stephenson, Alan Agar, John Bates and even Jeff missed two games due to knocks. In the 14 points all draw at McLaren Field, Bramley, Dewsbury were forced to field a pack which included four reserve forwards, Harry Beverley, Keith Voyce, Brian Taylor, Steve Hankins, Greg Chalkley and John Clark.

The game against the touring Australians attracted a good gate at the old Crown Flatt. Jeff was back after missing the previous game at Bramley but John Bates and Joe Whittington were still injured. The game was full of incidents as the great Arthur Beetson put his mark on the match with some heavy tackles and some over enthusiastic high shots. Substitute forward Steve Hankins challenged the ultra tough Beetson, after one high tackle on Harry Beverley, but bravery alone was not enough and poor Steve was dispatched, via a stretcher, to the dressing room with concussion! Jeff introduced himself to the Aussies with a strong game in which his now trademark tackling was a feature. The result was a 17–3 win for the Aussies, heralding a respectful showing on Dewsbury's part considering the standard of opposition. Again Jeff's club form was consistently good and the newspapers repeatedly banged the drum for Jeff to be given a run for England or even Great

Britain.

Dewsbury took on Hull Kingston Rovers in the BBC2 Floodlit Trophy but the Robins were too good for them on the night and Dewsbury tumbled out of the competition 28–8. The team then began a hit-and-miss spell in their league fixtures as wins against Oldham (home 19–13), Widnes (away 17–10), Leigh (in a great home victory 21–10), Rochdale Hornets (home 10–5), Widnes (home 13–7) and Halifax (away in the John Player Trophy first round, 16–7) were mixed with several defeats. These defeats included Hull Kingston Rovers in the BBC2 Floodlit Trophy, Hull Kingston Rovers again in the league (away 28–7), St Helens (away 35–5) and Castleford (away 19–13).

After the good away win at Thrum Hall, Halifax in the John Player Trophy, Dewsbury took on Leeds at Crown Flatt on the day before Christmas Eve. This was a real tester for the Dewsbury boys as it was the first time since the Championship win that Leeds had visited Crown Flatt. On the day, Leeds were at their almost untouchable best and scored five tries through Les Dyl 2, Alan Hardisty 2 and John Atkinson with Dave Marshall kicking two goals. Dewsbury's reply was a try by Alan Agar and three Nigel Stephenson goals in the 19–9 win for Leeds. Heavy defeats followed at The Willows, Salford and at Wilderspool against Warrington. Two victories, both at home, against Castleford and Hull Kingston Rovers eased the slight fall in league position but then following another sound 26–9 defeat at the hands of Leeds at Headingley saw the start of the Challenge Cup with a first round draw against New Hunslet at Crown Flatt. Tries by Greg Ashcroft, Terry Day and Keith Voyce with two Nigel Stephenson goals sent Dewsbury through to round two and another stiff game against Workington Town at Derwent Park. In between the cup rounds

Dewsbury had two tough league games against Whitehaven away (won 8–7) and Wigan at home.

For the Wigan game Dewsbury rested one or two players and had Nigel Stephenson missing with a facial injury sustained in the Leeds game. The backs for the Wigan game looked most unusual and the players selected were John Maloney; Gary Mitchell, John Clark, Terry Day, Greg Ashcroft; Alan Agar and Steve Lee. The pack looked strong enough with all the regular forwards on show. Wigan were in the process of rebuilding their great side and had few of their old guard left in the team but they proved too strong for Dewsbury on the day and the Wiganers powered through to a 9–2 win despite excellent games by Jeff, John Bates and Greg Chalkley.

The cup game at Workington was a typically torrid affair with Rushton back in the full back spot, Maloney in the centre for Clark and the half backs, Lee and Alan Bates. Jeff remembers, 'Any cup tie away from home is a battle, this one was more physical than most and we knew we would have to stand our corner to win it'. The pack was, as one would expect for that tough away cup tie, Beverley, Voyce, Lowe, Grayshon, John Bates and Chalkley. Workington knew the easiest way to beat Dewsbury was to niggle them and get them fighting. Their game plan was to upset the machine like flow of Tommy Smales's forward set pieces and nullify the Yorkshire men's fluent back division by knocking them about in the tackle. This tactic was not new by any means and against some lesser teams it worked and made life easier for the Cumbrians.

But the Dewsbury pack, with Jeff and John Bates to the fore and supported well by the granite hard Harry Beverley and the crafty experience of Dick Lowe, would not be intimidated and they simply carried on with the excellent game plan of coach Smales. That day Dewsbury had Steve Lee at stand off for the injured Alan Agar and Steve's tough, no nonsense attitude was just what was needed in this game. John Maloney too, in the centre for the injured Nigel Stephenson, was the strong, experienced player required for this type of game. John had a great depth of knowledge from his many seasons playing for Hull FC. So Dewsbury travelled to the North West coast with the correct grounding to do well. The game was exactly as they envisaged it would be, high shots, late tackles, gangs of two or three tacklers tearing in and stopping the runners dead in their tracks. It was a real old fashioned cup tie with no quarter asked nor given. The two big, strong running forwards, Jeff and Harry Beverley smashed their way over for tries. John Maloney landed three goals and Dick Lowe landed one goal in this extra hard 14–4 cup win for Dewsbury. As Jeff said, 'They didn't come any harder than Workington at Derwent Park. The yarns and tales about Cumberland forwards being tough came true in this cup tie, they were big and mean and determined to win'.

Through now to the crucial third round of the Challenge Cup, the key players at Dewsbury remembered the same stage from the previous season when Wakefield Trinity came to Crown Flatt in round three. Jeff recalls:

> This round is make or break . . . Win it and you are only 90 minutes away from Wembley. Loose it and it is a 12 month wait before you get another chance. All the lads who had been involved last season in the semi final against Bradford Northern knew what was expected especially Tommy Smales who had walked the same path with Featherstone Rovers when they beat Barrow at Wembley. Whoever we faced in round three we had to be ready.

The draw was made on TV and the balls came out with Dewsbury to play Leeds at Crown Flatt. 'If we want to go all the way, then we have to beat Leeds to get to London,' said Jeff.

In between the second and third rounds of the cup, Dewsbury had to play Warrington away. Typical of Tommy Smales, he selected his strongest side to travel to Wilderspool. No one rested: 'Just go out and beat Warrington, the Leeds cup tie will look after itself,' was Tommy's philosophy. Despite a great effort Dewsbury lost to Warrington by 26–10.

On Sunday 10 March Leeds came to Crown Flatt confident they could repeat the previous three meetings of the two clubs and march into the semi final game which was to be played 13 days later.

Leeds had beaten Batley away and Salford at home in the previous rounds and had gone eight games without defeat. No one fancied Dewsbury and the general opinion was that Leeds were going to be too strong and fast for the home team to handle. By restricting Leeds to one penalty goal kicked by David Marshall and with unbelievable tenacity and brute strength, Dewsbury once again tackled their hearts out to deny Leeds a try in the whole game. On the other hand Greg Chalkley, a very fast and elusive loose forward, had latched onto the final pass of a Tommy Smales move to break clear and zoom over for a fine try. Nigel Stephenson kicked three superb goals to give the heroes of Crown Flatt a magnificent 9–2 victory and back to back Challenge Cup Semi Finals. Dewsbury's 'in your face' defence was too much for the Leeds star spangled side who could not get their fast backs into action against the flat, quick moving defence. All the forwards played wonderfully well and the backs supported the pack manfully. What made this victory so sweet was the fact that in the County Cup and the two league matches already played before the Challenge Cup game, Leeds had scored 75 points against

Dewsbury's 23. The *Yorkshire Evening Post* gave great credit to the Dewsbury side:

> Leeds were made to look slow and pedestrian against this tackling machine that Tommy Smales has formed at Crown Flatt. It was like the tide crashing against the sea wall. The clever moves used by the Dewsbury pack when in possession must have taken hours in practice to attain such perfection and timing of passing and handling.

So just two weeks short of a year, Dewsbury were again 80 minutes away from a visit to Wembley. Bradford Northern had been their opponents in the previous season, but this time the strong Warrington side stood in the way to cup glory. Jeff well remembers the feeling during the approach to the semi final:

> We had a great spirit in the club and we knew that this Warrington side would be even harder to beat than the one in the previous season in the Championship semi final and that was one of the hardest games we had ever played in. The fact that Alex Murphy had left himself out of the Warrington side made us think that he considered this game as a walk over and we wanted to prove him wrong.

But it was another heartbreaker for Jeff and his Dewsbury team mates as the well oiled Warrington machine won the game 17–7. To be honest the score flattered Dewsbury as The Wire were stronger, faster and more aware than Dewsbury on the day. The Crown Flatt forwards were second best as Warrington's mighty six out-thought and out-muscled Dewsbury's slightly smaller pack. Speaking many years later to Warrington's captain on the day, Kevin Ashcroft, about this game Kevin recalls:

Dewsbury were always a hard team to beat as they never gave up any game without a huge fight. This semi final was no different. If anything they were not as dangerous when carrying the ball as they were with Mick Stephenson at hooker. He made them tick in big games and being without his drive and footballing expertise was a body blow to them when playing against top opposition such as Warrington. I remember in this particular game that whilst Jeff Grayshon, John Bates and Harry Beverley stood their ground and offered strong resistance, Alex Murphy, our coach, had targeted Dewsbury's three quarter line as being a little inexperienced in Challenge Cup football. He focused our attacking forwards to aim at them instead of taking on Grayshon and company down the middle of the field. Wanbon, Nicholas, Barry Philbin and big Aussie Dave Wright had run throughout the game at Terry Day, Gary Mitchell, Nigel Stephenson and Greg Ashcroft and gradually the Dewsbury midfield defence began to open up a wee bit. Moving the ball wider than normal for us proved the tactics absolutely spot on.

The League Championship was now the only trophy to play for and there were still seven games in which to aim for a home draw in the play offs. Four of these games were tough away fixtures, Wigan, Wakefield Trinity, Featherstone Rovers and Rochdale Hornets. The remaining home fixtures were Salford, Bramley and Warrington. Salford arrived at Crown Flatt with their star studied three quarters and in an exciting game Dewsbury won 14–10.

Eight days after the semi final, Dewsbury produced a terrific performance to beat Warrington 31–18. Jeff had a memorable game scoring a long range try and leading his team in a frantic effort to erase the mediocre semi final memory. Jeff's display was noted by several County selectors as well as a couple of the international board who were present at the game. The following day Dewsbury travelled to Central Park, Wigan and were brought down to earth with a bang. Completely run off their feet, Dewsbury were crushed 41–10 on April Fool's Day. To be fair the ravages of a hard fixture list had played havoc with the normally strong Crown Flatt pack. Missing from the semi final forwards were the experienced Dick Lowe, the tough Harry Beverley and the consistently good John Bates. Graham Bell, Keith Voyce, Steve Hankins, Jeff Grayshon, Grahame Chalkley and John Clark were the forwards on the day and the fact that the Dewsbury subs were two backs, John Russell and Steve Lee supports the fact that there were several injuries to the regular team.

For the Bramley game at Crown Flatt Bernard Gray came in for Adrian Rushton at full back, and with the return of Beverley and Lowe the pack seemed more evenly balanced with Harry Beverley, Ronnie Barham, Dick Lowe, Jeff Grayshon, Steve Hankins and John Clark. The result was a hard fought 11–3 victory for Dewsbury. Three away games faced the Dewsbury players as the season rapidly ended. The hard as nails Featherstone Rovers at Post Office Road was the first and just one change emerged from the Bramley win, that of Phil Smith on the wing for Greg Ashcroft and young Mick Bastin on the bench as forward sub. Again Jeff was the top forward as his pace and power allowed him to smash through Rovers defence to set up a try by Nigel Stephenson. Two days later, Dewsbury travelled the short distance to Belle Vue, Wakefield to take on Trinity. A 10–3 defeat awaited them as Jeff again played an outstanding game and registered a fine solo try. Another two days passed before Dewsbury drove across the Pennines to tackle one of the hardest teams to beat on their own ground, Rochdale Hornets. Dewsbury welcomed back the hard working John Bates at loose forward. Hard as they tried the Hornets proved just too strong for Dewsbury and went on to win 13–11. The play off first round took

Dewsbury back to Belle Vue where, again, Trinity proved too good for them with a 26–11 win and sent Dewsbury tumbling out of the competition.

Jeff, after feeling uneasy for a few weeks, considered asking for a move to another club. He and Dewsbury chairman, Mr Mick Lumb, met and Jeff asked to be put on the club's transfer list. Obviously Mick Lumb wanted to keep the in-form county forward and explained that he would have to ask a considerable sum should Jeff insist on being transfer listed. Jeff had made his mind up that a change of club would be beneficial to him so the club put him on open to transfer for a fee of £16,000.

There were some rays of sunshine for the club even though they won no trophies. The two Bates brothers, John and Alan were notified that they had both gained selection on the 1974 tour of Australia and New Zealand. Unfortunately a severe head injury to John, sustained in the seventh game on tour, forced him to return home. John Bates, a cornerstone of the excellent Dewsbury pack, played only 22 further games for the club before retiring totally.

3

INTERNATIONALS

The author remembers the start of the 1974–75 season vividly. I had been selected to replace Tommy Smales as Dewsbury's senior coach after Tommy had moved on to take over at his home town club of Featherstone Rovers. One or two of the 'old guard' players thought my approach a little too forthright and by all accounts complained to the committee. Not Jeff. He was a phlegmatic character and little got him down. My first senior coaching job at Dewsbury lasted just six games before I was shown the door but life goes on and Jeff, along with Alan and John Bates and Greg Chalkley did their utmost for my cause. Defeats by Featherstone Rovers, St Helens, Salford and Bradford Northern in the John Player Trophy, and then by Castleford and Warrington led to a change of coach. As usually happens, after losing those six games the same team won the following fixture against Bradford Northern in the league and indeed, with Jeff leading the pack in great style, gained two historic victories in November beating Warrington 11–10 and Wigan 14–5, both at Crown Flatt.

But early in the season on 11th September, Jeff and John Bates were selected together in the second row to play for Yorkshire in the re-vamped County Championship. Wales had pulled out of the European Championship and this enabled the selectors to call on the Welshmen to form a strong Other Nationalities team to compete in the County Championship. Yorkshire played Cumbria at Derwent Park, Workington in their first game and after the first league game of the season the Rugby Football League called a halt to the league fixtures to play these County games, all held mid week.

Yorkshire Versus Cumbria, Derwent Park, Workington, 11 September 1974

The sparse crowd witnessed a competitive game with the two packs going at it hammer and tongs. Jeff picked up from David Topliss to make several long runs and his midfield defence was as strong as usual. One powerful break by Jeff was continued by Steve Norton who put David Hartley over for Yorkshire's only try. The result went Cumbria's way with a 10–7 win. Brian Jefferson kicked two goals to go with Hartley's try and the speedy Paul Charlton scored two tries for Cumbria with Graham Mather kicking two goals.

There were still two games left to play in this competition but in the days of County selection it was a lottery depending on whether one was the flavour of the month or not. This County Championship was played without a break with no league fixtures interfering with the competition. Yorkshire's second game was against the Other Nationalities team.

Yorkshire Versus Other Nationalities, Craven Park, Hull, 18 September 1974

This unusual fixture produced a cracking display with fast attacking football that had the reporter of the *Hull Daily Mail* suggesting that this was the best County Championship game ever seen:

The clashes between the two packs was worth the admission alone. Mostly violent tackling ensued from the start and the Yorkshire forwards although giving as much as they were taking, gradually produced a more balanced attack with strong rushes then quick movement out to the backs. There was some fine play from Thompson [Featherstone], Grayshon [Dewsbury] and Norton [Castleford] with Bates [Dewsbury] and Burton [Halifax] two extremely constructive half backs. The aggressive play of Mills [Widnes], Fisher [Leeds] and Butler [Swinton] had earned the Other Nationalities a 15–8 lead at half time but in the second half the pace of the White Rose team in midfield gradually eased the fire out of the visiting team and thanks to tries by Redfearn [Bradford Northern], Smith [Featherstone Rovers] Atkinson [Leeds] and Burton [Halifax] plus five goals by Marshall [Leeds] gave Yorkshire the victory with 22 points. Tries by Barends [York], Diabira [Bradford Northern] and Dixon [Salford] and three goals by Wilkins [Blackpool Borough] tallied up to the 15 points scored by Other Nationalities.

So Yorkshire were up and running having to pull back a win after the shock defeat in Cumbria. Lancashire had beaten both Other Nationalities, 14–13 at the Willows, Salford and Cumbria 29–4 at Wilderspool, Warrington and were solid favourites to take the Championship. The key game for Yorkshire was the 'derby' game against Lancashire. A tradition in these inter County games was to select at least one player from the club hosting the game. In this game chances were given to two promising young Keighley players, centre Peter Roe and hooker Dean Raistrick.

Yorkshire Versus Lancashire, Lawkholme Lane, Keighley, 25 September 1974

Yorkshire set about their task in good style with Jeff and Bob Irving running well off the expert ball handling of Roger

Millward and Steve Norton. But Lancashire, cock-a-hoop after consecutive wins, had confidence in their own ability and although Dave Marshall landed two early penalty goals the Red Rose outfit crossed for two outstanding tries by Chris Hesketh and the excellent Tommy Martyn. With Derek Whitehead kicking four goals, Lancashire went in at half time 14–4 ahead. Jeff recalls:

> We had a good talk at half time and decided to use myself and Bob Irving on a couple of simple moves near their line and pass the ball wider to use the pace of Roger Millward and John Atkinson. We also talked about tightening the defence and this is where the enthusiastic Graham Idle came into his own. Graham tackled his heart out in that second half and his example set us on a good defensive display.

The second half saw a transformation within the Yorkshire side as their defence tightened considerably and Bob Irving's power and pace brought him a try from one of the set piece moves from a close-in play the ball. Moving the ball wide at every opportunity, Yorkshire cashed in with three excellent tries from John Atkinson, Roger Millward and Alan Bates. John Bates came on as a substitute to form that extra tight defence and work well with Jeff on attack. David Marshall obliged with another two goals and with their outstanding defence holding out this half, Yorkshire marched to a 20–14 victory.

The County Championship proved to be a close affair that season as Cumbria, Lancashire and Yorkshire were level on the same points. This meant that the play off game had to be decided on points scored for and against. As it was, Lancashire had the best aggregate with 57 points for and 37 against whilst Yorkshire were in second place with 49 points for and 39 against.

Lancashire Versus Yorkshire County Championship Final, Naughton Park, Widnes, 16 October 1974

Lancashire were determined to capture the County Championship in this decider. The Warrington contingent of Noonan, Gordon, Chisnall, Ashcroft, Brady and Philbin proved too strong and pacey for the Yorkshire men and by half time had the game won, leading 18–6. George Nicholls played exceptionally well for Lancashire and led their pack in fine style according to the newspaper reporters present at the game. Kevin Ashcroft remembers the game vividly and can recall most of the important events:

> Yorkshire started like a house on fire. What kept us in the game early on was that I managed to take several early scrums against Dean Raistrick. With big Mal Dixon bringing his fast moving back three on to his short passes we had all on containing Jeff Grayshon, Bob Irving and Steve Norton. Big Jeff, in particular, took some holding. Both teams were hungry for that beautiful gold winners medal which without doubt was one of the nicest medals to play for. Jeff Grayshon was a very strong man who made every ounce of his big frame count as he made a tackle. He also ran strongly into any gap that appeared in your defensive line. He was a good 'un.

Gradually Lancashire began to dominate and the Lancashire backs took advantage of the forwards' supremacy by scoring all the home side's five tries. Derek Noonan (2), Stewart Wright, Chris Hesketh and Kenny Gill crossed the whitewash with Ray Dutton bang on goal kicking form with seven goals. Peter Roe, John Atkinson and Steve Norton crossed for Yorkshire and Bruce Burton landed one goal meaning Lancashire collected the trophy with a final score of 29–11. Jeff played well enough to have his name placed in the County selectors' notebooks for the future and one or two of the bigger clubs were beginning to take notice of this well built, fast back rower who had proved to be one of the big pluses for Yorkshire in this inter County Championship.

The beginning of the 1974–75 season was not a happy one for the club. The first six games ended in defeat and after the eighth game of the season Dewsbury had tumbled out of the Yorkshire Cup, the John Player Trophy and the BBC2 Floodlit Trophy competition, in fact they only won five of the first 21 games. One of the problems was the injury crisis at the club plus one or two players were disgruntled with the results and were staying away from the club. Jeff played in 31 of Dewsbury's 35 matches and his form was consistently good enough to maintain his position in the County pack for the following season. Despite the poor general league and cup performances Dewsbury did have one or two brighter moments with excellent wins against Bradford Northern 15–14, Warrington 11–10, Wigan 14–5, Wakefield Trinity 20–13, Widnes 31–7, Halifax 28–18 and Salford 17–16, all these games being at Crown Flatt. Dewsbury's only away win was at Belle Vue, Wakefield where they beat Trinity 17–5.

The 1975–76 season was a busy time for Jeff in his rugby career. The magic call to advise on selection for England came by letter in late August and coincided with Dewsbury's good start to the season. Wins against Huddersfield and Wakefield Trinity at home and Keighley away in the league were followed by a cracking 7–3 win over Wakefield Trinity again, this time in the BBC2 Floodlit Trophy at Crown Flatt.

Then came a big day for Jeff when he took the field at Wilderspool Stadium, Warrington for the England Versus Wales game in the 1975 World Championship competition held from September to November in England, New Zealand and

France. It was a great day for Jeff, wife Sue and son Paul, in fact for all the Grayshon family. The nations competing in this World Championship were France, Wales, New Zealand, Australia and England. England v Wales kicked off the competition.

England Versus Wales, World Championship, Wilderspool Stadium, Warrington, 20 September 1975

This first game of the tournament was as exciting as the score suggests with England the eventual 22–16 winners. Jeff played to his outstanding club form and was one of the England successes. Keith Fielding, John Holmes and Eric Hughes scored tries for England with Keith Bridges dropping a goal and George Fairbairn landing six goals. Jeff had a hand in Fielding's try with a good break and feed out to the supporting Hughes who handed on to his wing partner to score. The sports writers mentioned Jeff repeatedly in their reports as 'a fine defensive player, strong in the head on tackle and a superb cover defender'. Wales answered the England scores with tries to Peter Banner and Kel Coslett with the Welsh captain Dai Watkins landing five goals.

Jeff was pleased with his debut as an England player commenting:

> To play for England was a great ambition of mine ever since I signed for Dewsbury. To be lucky enough to play well was a huge bonus and I only hoped my performance was going to be good enough to keep me in the team.

On the other side of the world, Australia took on New Zealand at Carlaw Park, Auckland in their first game in the competition. The Aussies won 24–8. Two weeks later, on 11 October in Bordeaux, England took on France. England went with the same team that had beaten Wales with the exception of John Atkinson who was unavailable. Ged Dunn, the excellent try scoring Hull Kingston Rovers player, came into the vacated wing position. Bordeaux was not a happy hunting ground for England and with the close result in the recent England v Wales game the French saw this opener in their own country as a great chance to cause an upset and start the competition in good style. They selected a tough, strong side and prepared well. The referee for this game was the experienced Mr John Percival of Auckland, New Zealand. Fourteen days earlier at Carlaw Park, Auckland, Australia had beaten New Zealand 24–8 in their competition opener in the Southern Hemisphere. France needed this win over England to keep in touch with the Aussies and England in this World Championship league.

England Versus France, Bordeaux, 11 October 1975

The English sports writers were ecstatic in their praise of this England performance. They raved about the work rate of the England forwards, particularly the speed and strength of Jeff, Bob Irving and Steve Norton. Jeff thrived on the ball play of Kenny Gill and Roger Millward, running onto their short delayed passes. The defensive work of England's forwards in general was praised as another key factor in the victory. The great lead from the in-form pack allowed the English backs acres of field to run in and no one benefited more than Keith Fielding who sped over for four tries showing his electric pace. John Holmes and Ged Dunn registered two tries each and Eric Hughes, Kenny Gill, Brian Hogan and Colin Forsyth forced themselves onto the try scoring list, George Fairbairn kicked four goals and Roger Millward two goals in this 48–2 massacre leaving the French selectors bemused and bewildered. Six days later at the Stade Velodrome in Marseilles, France and New Zealand drew 12 points apiece. It was another bad result for the home country but the interesting point in this game was the attendance, 26,879.

Suddenly the effort required to win this competition became clear. Australia defeated Wales at St Helens then at Swansea by 18–6 on 19th October and had two games to play, the first against France in Perpignan on the same day that England and New Zealand met. In the New Zealand game at Odsal Stadium, Bradford on 26th October, England had three enforced changes with Keith Fielding, Bob Irving and Dave Eckersley dropping out through injury and replaced by Stuart Wright, Mick Adams and Les Dyl.

England Versus New Zealand, Odsal Stadium, Bradford, 26 October 1975

England beat New Zealand 27–12 in a professional display. Star of the show was Kenny Gill who scored a hat trick of tries by simply following his big forwards who created the gaps into which Gill ran. Stuart Wright, Ged Dunn and Eric Hughes along with Steve Norton added touchdowns and George Fairbairn kicked three goals. For New Zealand James Smith and Alan Gordon scored tries and Warren Collicoat landed three goals.

On the same day the Aussies beat France 41–2 in Perpignan to set up a Winner-Takes-All final at Central Park, Wigan on 1st November. This victory was the one the English supporters wanted in revenge after England lost the ashes in the recent close Test series in Australia. The Australians had relished the Test series and wanted to register another win over the old country in this championship. The Rugby Football League produced a good presentation of this final and it was well publicised throughout with adverts on TV and in the national newspapers. The attendance of 10,000 was disappointing to say the least. But putting all behind them the England team had developed a fine team spirit and a tough will to win attitude and the players were in determined mood as match day approached.

England Versus Australia,
Central Park, Wigan, 1 November 1975

Australia had a strong, aggressive side containing players who would be classed later as all time greats such as Arthur Beetson, Graham Eadie, Mick Cronin, Johnny Peard, Terry Randall and Steve Rogers. The Green and Golds really fancied themselves to win this competition and selected their strongest and most in-form team.

England were forced to swap several players from the New Zealand win owing to injuries. Les Dyl and David Redfearn formed a new centre-wing partnership and Jimmy Thompson, the great forward of Featherstone, was in for Colin Forsyth. Bob Irving, back after injury, returned to the second row with Mick Adams going onto the bench as substitute along with Eric Hughes. Reports in the local newspapers told of five star performances from Steve Norton, Jimmy Thompson and Jeff Grayshon. Jeff's contribution, besides tackling his heart out and working with an almost ferocious appetite, was in scoring one of England's two tries. John Holmes scored the other try in this 16–13 win for England and George Fairbairn kicked five goals to the hat trick of tries by Ian Schubert and two goals by Mick Cronin for Australia.

In those days international games with Australia were tight affairs. On the 1974 Lions tour, the first Test went Australia's way 12–6, the Lions won the second Test 16–11 and Australia won the deciding Test 22–18, nothing in it at all. So recent Test history was proved correct as this cracking World Championship final at Wigan provided a thrilling and massively entertaining finale to a successful tournament. As the competition lasted 43 days, the everyday business of running the Rugby Football League continued normally. Most of the players doubled up the day after the international game by playing for their club. Jeff missed only the Castleford home game throughout the whole competition, a game Dewsbury won 20–12. This was because of travelling to play the French in Bordeaux on the same day.

So ended Jeff's superbly successful first taste of international football. He had in his collection of medals a winners medal from this World International Championship. Apart from owning a magnificent medal, Jeff had confirmed and cemented his place as an international forward at the age of 26. For a player who started late his progress was phenomenal. Jeff's natural strength and fitness helped his progress and his work as a brick drawer built up this natural strength giving him the perfect physique for a back row forward. As he approached his thirties he also reached his full power and his size and experience gained him further notoriety as a front rower of exceeding ability.

The 1975–76 season, as well as including the World Championship, gave all clubs the opportunity to enter four major cup competitions, the Challenge Cup, County Cup, John Player Trophy and BBC2 Floodlit Trophy. The end of season Premiership Trophies were played separately by teams at the top of the two divisions. Dewsbury won ten league games and drew one out of 30 played. In the first round of the County Cup game, Jeff was in the second row in this 18–12 defeat by York at Clarence Street. In the John Player Trophy, Widnes beat Dewsbury 27–12 in the first round at Naughton Park. York also beat Dewsbury 25–15 in the first round of the Challenge Cup, again on the York ground. In the BBC2 Floodlit Trophy, Dewsbury excelled. Jeff scored his side's only try in the 7–3 win over Wakefield Trinity at Crown Flatt in round one. In round two, Dewsbury entertained Keighley and won comfortably enough 22–10. On 2nd November Dewsbury played Oldham at the Watersheddings in a league game and lost 15–6. On Tuesday 11th November Dewsbury again visited Oldham in the third round of the BBC2 Floodlit Trophy and a terrific defensive performance saw them through to win 11–9.

Jeff had to perform a quick mental switch over after the Oldham away game as the following evening he was invited to represent England against Australia at Headingley in an international game that was not counted as a full international. Two of Jeff's team mates, Harry Beverley and Nigel Stephenson were rewarded for their consistently good club form and invited to play for England. Australia were still smarting over the defeat by England in the World Championship and were determined to gain revenge for this surprising defeat. With the Australians still in this country from the competition the game would also add to the financial side of this championship for the Aussies.

England Versus Australia, Headingley, Leeds, 12 November 1975

The 25–0 defeat inflicted by the Aussies was to say the least expected. The introduction of the BBC2 Floodlit Trophy was in essence a great innovation. Played on Tuesday evenings it captured the imagination of supporters and proved popular with the TV audience. But to work in another game on the Wednesday evening against a determined and classy

Australian outfit turned out to be disastrous. Jeff, Harry Beverley and Nigel Stephenson had played the evening before in the Floodlit game at Oldham and found it hard. Come half time, the England team had competed well enough to be only 8–0 down, but against strong opposition they had little left to throw at the Aussies. Tries by Mick Cronin, Johnny Peard, Terry Randall and two by hooker Johnny Lang plus five Graham Eadie goals meant the Green and Golds rattled up 25 points without reply. Fresh with no game from 1st November, the Australians set about the English pack as though it was a test match. With several players also making debuts in international football, the task proved too much and the result, regardless of circumstances, was a blow to fragile British confidence gained against the old enemy in the World Championship.

Back at Dewsbury, the results in the league took a dip after the great win at Oldham. Two home defeats against Featherstone Rovers 5–24 and Leeds 16–25 were followed by a defeat at Odsal against Bradford Northern 0–12. This was not great preparation, one would think, for the biggest game at Crown Flatt for a few years, the semi final of the BBC2 Floodlit Trophy against one of the favourites to win it, Leeds. Jeff recalls, 'We had to do something in this game as only 16 days earlier Leeds had won at Dewsbury and scored seven tries in doing so. Our tackling had to be much better in the cup game'.

Jeff had said that Dewsbury must defend better and they did. Led by a magnificent defensive performance by Jeff himself and followed by each Dewsbury player, the home side blotted out every Leeds move and took their chance when John Hegarty forced his way over to score a try converted by Nigel Stephenson who also dropped two goals. The end result, a 7–0 win for Dewsbury, saw them into the BBC2 Floodlit Trophy final against St Helens, at Knowsley Road on 16th December. Jeff remembers:

> It was a terrible evening with gale force winds blowing straight down the slope into the 'Nine Oil' (an area in the bottom right hand corner which had a huge dip in the ground which fell away to the corner flag). We played up the slope in the first half and we couldn't believe that Leeds hadn't used the wind to force us into our own 25. I never did much kicking for any of the clubs I played for but that evening I hoofed the ball into the Nine Oil every time we were in our own territory and we were not bothered if it simply went into dead ball. We played to keep Leeds at the bottom of the slope all that half and it worked.

Five days after the great win over Leeds it was back to league football and a strong Widnes team arrived at Crown Flatt. Widnes were going great guns in the league and had some exceptional key players in Reg Bowden, Jim Mills, Eric Hughes, Mick Adams and Keith Elwell. As it was, Widnes were too strong for the brave Dewsbury lads and won this game 19–1 (the point coming from a Nigel Stephenson drop goal). However, the Dewsbury team had other things on their mind as two days later they travelled to St Helens for the BBC2 Floodlit Trophy final.

Dewsbury Versus St Helens, BBC2 Floodlit Trophy Final, Knowsley Road, 16 December 1975

The final was played on a freezing evening and it was blatantly obvious that the Saints team wanted this cup. Dewsbury went into their most important game since the 1972–73 Championship Final without the in-form centre John Clark who took a knock against Widnes and was unfit. The speedy Greg Chalkley was moved from the second row to centre in place of John Clark and the grand utility forward, Graham Bell came in for Greg

Chalkley allowing Jeff to fill in at loose forward. Saints held all the aces in this game and did a very professional job on Dewsbury to lift the BBC2 Floodlit Trophy by a comfortable score of 22–2. Saints tries were scored by Roy Mathias (2), Dave Hull, Billy Benyon and Frank Wilson and Kel Coslett and Geoff Pimblett kicked the goals with Jeff Heaton dropping a goal.

After the BBC2 Floodlit Trophy final Dewsbury's 1975–76 season fell into decline except for two outstanding results against Leeds at Headingley and St Helens at Knowsley Road. Jeff had played against Leeds three times that season, twice in the league and once in the BBC2 Floodlit Trophy. Dewsbury lost at Headingley in the league game 25–16. Jeff's side beat Leeds in the BBC2 Floodlit Trophy 7–0.

Dewsbury were on a six game losing run. In fact, Jeff recalls:

We were in a poor run and hadn't won a game since we beat Leeds in the BBC2 Floodlit Trophy game. We knew the answer lay with us, the team, so we could be boosted by a good performance at Headingley. And what a turn up, we set about Leeds from the kick off and young Welsh scored a close in try. Gary Mitchell did well to score his try which was followed by John Langley linking into the three quarters and racing over, Phil Artis kicked two goals and we had 13 points. But Leeds were a grand side and Neil Hague, Phil Cookson and Kevin Dick scored in quick succession and with Dave Marshall kicking two goals the score was tied at 13 points all. In the closing minutes our pack drove to the Leeds posts and someone called out, 'Drop a goal Jeff!', so I took a pass and pop, I must have hit it right because the ball flew over the crossbar for the winning point and we came away from Headingley with a 14–13 win!

In the other almost unbelievable win at St Helens on 9th April, one has to accept that Dewsbury had run Saints all the way at Crown Flatt in the League being beaten in the final few minutes by 7–6. The heavy defeat in the BBC2 Floodlit Trophy final may well have been because it was played on Saints home ground. This league game was at the end of a long, hard season for Jeff and his team mates and there may well have been a case for just turning up to fulfil the fixture. But Jeff and the Dewsbury team were more professional than that and the team went seeking revenge for the BBC2 Floodlit Trophy defeat.

Unfortunately, winning only three games after the defeat by Saints in the BBC2 Floodlit Trophy final, Dewsbury had had a poor season. Injuries had a lot to do with the decline and the amount of games key players missed was a factor in the disappointing season. Yet despite his international and County call ups, Jeff played in 36 of the 38 games played by Dewsbury, a unique record and one that showed his tremendous tenacity and resolve, not to mention his physical and mental strength. Jeff also possessed a wonderful ability to recover from knocks and minor injuries, hence his record of playing so many consistent games. Those two games missed for his club were down to playing international football either in France or in home internationals on the same day as the club's fixtures.

In this disappointing 1975–76 season for his club, Jeff was still very active on the inter County scene. The season's County Championship games involving Yorkshire were to be played at Crown Flatt, Dewsbury, Central Park, Wigan and Odsal Stadium, Bradford. The game at Crown Flatt was against Cumbria, dangerous opponents at any time. The game was played on on a cold, damp Wednesday evening.

Cumbria Versus Yorkshire, Crown Flatt, Dewsbury, 19 November 1975

It was a struggle for both sides as the two defences were tight. Eddie Bowman the Workington Town sub forward was called on early because of an injury to key player Harry Marsland and Eddie introduced himself to the Yorkshire side by crashing over for a strong try just before half time and two Arnie Walker goals against one goal by John Holmes gave Cumbria a 7–2 half time lead. Yorkshire's pack came strong in the second half and Jeff's contribution was several long breaks which delighted the Dewsbury supporters out in force to cheer on their three club representatives, Jeff, Harry Beverley and Nigel Stephenson. David Smith went over for a try after great work by Bob Irving, Jeff and Les Dyl and John Holmes converted to make it 7–7. Then, following another fine run by Jeff, the home side moved the ball swiftly to John Holmes who went in at the corner for the winning try as Yorkshire triumphed 10–7. All three Dewsbury players who starred for the County that evening had played against Featherstone Rovers the previous Sunday and were on duty again on the following Sunday against Leeds, both games held at Crown Flatt.

The County Championship competition consisted of four teams, Yorkshire, Lancashire, Cumbria and Other Nationalities.

Yorkshire Versus Other Nationalities, Odsal Stadium, Bradford, 6 December 1975

Yorkshire's next game was against the unknown quantity Other Nationalities. Yorkshire made three changes from the team that beat Cumbria. Nigel Stephenson came from the bench to take over from Les Dyl in the centre, Steve Nash [Salford] took over from Roger Millward at half back and David Topliss [Wakefield Trinity] moved onto the bench as sub back. The Other Nationalities side was made up of overseas players plus some Welshmen, some of Irish and Scottish extraction and one or two who had no idea where they were from! Despite the lowly crowd of spectators, those in attendance saw a remarkable game in which the 'no hopers', the makeshift team of Other Nationalities, almost pulled off the win of the season and Yorkshire were relieved to come away with a 16–16 draw. It was one of those games where nothing went right for the Yorkshire team. Constantly driven back by the expert kicking of half back Steve Martin, Yorkshire made many chances but the terrific last ditch tackling and tremendous enthusiasm of the Other Nationalities held them in great stead. Hull Kingston Rovers full back Dickie Wallace scored two tries for Other Nationalities and scores by David Barands and Frank Wilson plus two goals by Harold Box gave the 'overseas' team their points. For Yorkshire tries by Jimmy Thompson (2), Keith Bridges, David Smith and two goals by John Holmes enabled the Yorkshire team a crucial share of the points.

Lancashire Versus Yorkshire, Central Park, Wigan, 20 December 1975

Lancashire had beaten Other Nationalities and Cumbria. Now only Yorkshire stood in the way of a prestigious win of this County Championship. Yorkshire had beaten Cumbria and drawn with the Other Nationalities. Should they lose to the Red Rose County then the chance of that superb gold medal would have gone, but if they could beat Lancashire then the championship would be theirs. Jeff recalls:

> The team were absolutely dejected after the draw at Odsal. We really wanted to win the championship that season. It meant a lot in those days to say you were County champions, the best County in English Rugby League. Quite a few of our players had never won one of those beautiful gold medals and in those days it was an honour to play for, and win for, Yorkshire. We said that if we were lucky enough to gain selection for this last

chance game then we would pull ourselves together and have a real go for it.

Those lucky enough to be selected were advised a week after the drawn game and the selections showed seven changes. Yorkshire played with real determination from the start and, as Jeff remembers:

> Everyone in the side pulled more than their weight in this game. Our backs were quick with Dave Topliss, Gary Stephens, John Holmes and Les Dyl in commanding form. Mick Morgan had an outstanding match scoring two tries and the pack as a whole were on top form from the start.

This fine win by Yorkshire brought the County Championship back to the broad acres and justified the County selectors' faith in the side. John Atkinson (1) and Mick Morgan (2) scored tries and John Holmes kicked four goals in the 17–7 win. A Sammy Turnbull try and two Ray Dutton goals gave Lancashire their points.

The League results made poor reading for Jeff and his team mates. In that 1975–76 season the Dewsbury club's playing record read played 30, won 10, drawn 1, lost 19. The promotion-relegation system in those days was four up, four down. The bottom four in the first division were relegated and the top four in the second division were promoted. This system unfortunately led to what became known as the Yo-Yo teams. Most of the teams promoted were too good for the second division and not quite good enough for the first division. Jeff found himself facing a season in the lower division as Dewsbury had finished in fourth from bottom place in the league ladder.

4

PLAYING DOWN UNDER

Several clubs had shown an interest in signing Jeff. Dewsbury let it be known that he was their biggest asset. They desperately wanted him to stay at Crown Flatt and would not consider a reduction of his transfer fee. This 1976–77 season saw Dewsbury produce a consistently good season losing only five of their 19 league matches. The season began brightly with victories in the Yorkshire Cup against Huddersfield at Fartown 26–18 in round one, followed by an excellent win in round two at Thrum Hall, Halifax by 26–14. Including the various cup games, amazingly Dewsbury played only six home games in the first 22 games of the season. A trip to Craven Park to play Hull Kingston Rovers in the first round of the BBC2 Floodlit Trophy saw the first defeat of the new season 19–12, then seven days later a 31–15 defeat at the hands of Leeds at Headingley sent them tumbling out of the Yorkshire Cup at the semi final stage. A run of six consecutive league wins came to a sudden and unexpected end when Huyton caused a surprise with a 16–2 upset at Alt Park. Jeff recalls this hiccup:

> We had started the season well with two Yorkshire Cup wins and a good performance at Hull Kingston in the BBC2 Floodlit Trophy, then a cracking win in a real hard game at home to Whitehaven by

10–5. So when Huyton turned us over it made us realise that we were not invincible in this division. A week later we came unstuck at McLaren Field in the John Player Trophy when Bramley cleaned us out in a 33–5 defeat. Whitehaven were the only side to beat us at Crown Flatt in the league when they came down and gave us another tough game beating us 7–3. But the most strange score we had was the win over York at home by 1–0! Nigel Stephenson's drop goal was the only score.

England Versus Wales, European Championship, Headingley, Leeds, 29 January 1977

The start of the European Championship was 29 January 1977 with an England v Wales game staged at Headingley. Jeff was informed of his selection and he was one of only two second division players in this international match. The other player was Huddersfield's Peter Rowe. Wales had on display some of the finest backs of that era and a big, tough, strong pack which would have intimidated even the world's strongest set of forwards. In a totally forward dominated game Wales took control from the first whistle. The powerful running of the likes of Mills, Mantle, Dixon and Nicholas had the England players forever on the back foot. When England did gain possession the Welsh tacklers were tiger-like in their attitude on defence. The home nation hardly created a chance against this brick wall tackling with Woods at scrum half playing with the strength and skill of an extra forward. Eddie Cunningham, again playing like an extra second rower, raced over for the only try of the game in mid second half, Woods converting and Peter Rowe adding a neat drop goal to give the Principality its six, which the only answer from England was a George Fairbairn penalty goal to give the result England 2 Wales 6. The repercussions of this event cost the international status of several players who had been regular selections in the recent past. Jeff was an exception as his defence during the whole of this game was exemplary. Covering almost every inch of ground he was one of only a few who came out of this game with his credibility intact.

Yorkshire Versus Cumbria,
Recreation Ground, Whitehaven, 15 February 1977

Jeff's selection for Yorkshire to play Cumbria up in Whitehaven on 15 February gave him his ninth County cap. Always a tough place to visit, no matter which team you were playing for, the Whitehaven ground, tight and surrounded by fiercely partisan Cumbrian supporters, was no place for a faint heart. This County fixture against Yorkshire always produced memorable battles with exiting incidents and was remembered for years by those who witnessed the games.

This particular inter County Championship game was full of such incidents with a crowd pleasing, tough, no holds barred encounter that had a touch of everything. Possibly it was because the County Championship competition was the only set of games, other than the Aussie, Kiwi or French international matches, that a supporter could cheer and shout for his personal County choice. The Cumbrian supporters were vocal in their enthusiasm for their home County. Selecting a strong side, which included two Whitehaven players in the 15 man squad, the Cumbrian players were determined to redeem themselves for the close 18–14 defeat by Lancashire two weeks before at Hilton Park, Leigh. Yorkshire also realised the importance of this game and selected a good, workman like side. The game developed into a clash of the two fine packs of forwards. Bowman, Flynn and Gorley were outstanding for Cumbria with Jeff Grayshon, Thompson and Morgan grafting for Yorkshire. When the ball was moved into the backs both sides were impressive. Charlton, running at every opportunity, as usual, into his team's three quarter moves, strode through for a typical majestic try and was followed by a strong Wilkins touchdown plus three goals from the accurate MacCorquodale. Yorkshire hit back with tries by Joiner and Topliss and three goals for Lloyd to give a score of 12 points all and secured a creditable draw for both sides in an excellent and totally absorbing County Championship game.

Dewsbury regained division one status gaining promotion in second place behind Hull FC in the 1976–77 season and Jeff's contribution to the promotion was that he played in every game for his club except in the home game against Halifax on 6th March. Jeff finished as Dewsbury's top try scoring forward with six tries. It was pleasing to have gained promotion in the first season and there was another bonus for Jeff when he was contacted by a gentleman from the Castleford area who asked if Jeff would be interested in taking his family to Australia and play a short season contract for one of Sydney's top clubs. The move was to be assisted by the then chairman of Castleford who would sort out all the details and let Jeff know in a meeting soon after.

Jeff and wife Sue went across to Castleford and met the club chairman. He told them that Cronulla were interested in him. The club is situated just outside Sydney and the deal would include a job and a super apartment overlooking the Pacific Ocean. Cronulla had several international players on their playing register and a couple who would be at that high level in the near future. Of the players there Jeff knew Paul Khan, the big prop forward who starred at Castleford, the classy international centre Steve Rogers, a top back rower in international games, Greg Pierce, Andrew Ettingshausen a brilliant young centre who was to become a real star of the future and the experienced Kiwi international forward, Dane Sorenson. Another British player had recently joined the Aussie club, David Eckersley from St Helens. If Jeff and Sue decided to go on this short contract, Jeff would have to swing it with the Dewsbury committee.

Jeff had requested a transfer earlier in his career and the club had listed him at a then record fee for a forward. Understandably Jeff thought it may be a tough ask for Dewsbury to allow a current Great Britain player to go to Australia in the close season. He said:

> I had quietly asked a few times if the club could arrange a transfer for me, thinking that because of my fairly regular selection in the national side one of the big clubs might be interested. Despite offers from Leeds, Hull Kingston Rovers and Oldham, the fee required by Dewsbury was a huge block in any sort of deal. In an effort to put me at ease again with the club, the committee suggested that I should become player-coach with the club and by promoting me to coach they could officially increase my wages. So I entered the unusual world of coaching. I gained an audience with the committee and explained that if I did accept the short contract from Cronulla it would only be for the summer close season here in the UK. I added that I would be back as soon as possible to lead the club again next season. Out of the blue the committee agreed and drew up a list of their requirements to send to Cronulla. Once this was arranged, Sue and I made the decision to go to the sun and good living land of Oz.

Jeff and Sue arranged for young Paul to have an extended summer holiday from school and the family were all set for a great adventure. Jeff spoke to as many British players as he could think of who had been out to play in Australia and was given some sound advice as to how the Aussies expected a Pom to behave in their country. Sue remembers the wonderful expectations the family had in going on an extended stay to the sunshine land.

Jeff and I were both young and inexperienced in travelling such a long way from home. We had never flown before so one can realise how we felt when we boarded the Qantas giant aircraft. On arrival in Sydney we were transported out to Cronulla and what a gorgeous place it was. Brilliant silver sand almost outside our apartment door and the superbly blue Pacific with the white breakers. Very different to our home in Birstall!

The people at Cronulla helped to settle Jeff, Sue and Paul. They arranged a job for Jeff in a timber yard and as the blokes there were all Cronulla supporters they thought working with Jeff was great. Jeff signed a short term contract with the club including perks such as a car and the apartment. The car was a little green 'Herbie'. Jeff recalls:

Sue hit it off well with Paul Khan's wife and spent time with her and her sons during the day when I was at work. Young Paul was around the same age as the Khan's sons and this meant that they quickly became the best of friends. On Cronulla beach there was a purpose made swimming area formed by large rocks. Sue and Paul were swimming one morning when Sue noticed a big sign saying 'DANGER—Beware of Blue Ringed Octopuses'. Sue was concerned that she and Paul could be in danger so they both swam over to a group of ladies sat on the rocks, dangling their feet in the water. Sue asked, 'Excuse me, what are Blue Ringed Octopuses?' With a shriek the ladies were out of the water immediately!

'Have you seen one?' they asked looking worried. Sue replied that she had just seen the sign and wanted to know what they were.

'Sweety, if one stings you you're in big trouble as you'll only have a few moments to get treatment!' explained one lady.

Jeff was asked to attend training at the Cronulla ground his first Tuesday in Australia. No one had warned him about the intense physical training programme that was in practice at the club.

> I had trained under some trainer-coaches I thought were total sadists at Dewsbury. But I had never been subjected to such physical and psychological pressure as those training sessions in Australia. The coach at the club was the much respected Ted Glossop, a nice bloke who obviously knew the game inside out. Under Ted were his training staff, conditioners who looked after the fitness side, skills coaches who covered every aspect of passing and handling, tackling, kick and chase and the stats men keeping Ted informed of who was working to his full potential and who was not.
>
> But as I entered the caldron that was Australian Rugby League, I realised exactly why the training was so brutal. There is no doubt that the Aussies are that much fitter than our players simply because their game is so much more physical than ours. In my career I have been stopped by some of the toughest tacklers in our game but only once ever have I been hit so hard that it made me feel ill and vomit. That was in a game against Canterbury Bankstown when I was almost cut into two with the perfect hit by one of our opponent's second rowers. I was completely knocked over, sideways, by a tackler's shoulder hitting me just under my rib cage. This collision took every last breath from my body and I felt a sickness like never before or since. By all accounts I was driven about two yards sideways and landed with the tackler still driving into me with his shoulder and the final bang into the hard ground just about finished me off.
>
> As I gradually came around and started breathing again I managed to get back onto the field and narrowly avoided another smack from the same player. This time I saw him coming and stepped away from the contact area. He sailed past like a torpedo missing a ship, thankfully. Being the new boy on the block and a current Great Britain forward, may have tempted one or two

Aussie 'assassins' to have a go at me. All in all, apart from the much harder training and the occasional 'big hit' things were not much different to being at home, and anyway I was a big lad then and could look after myself.

But it was very different for Sue as she quickly became homesick. Sometimes sunshine and a home by the sea is not enough to make up for the company of family and near friends and Sue began to miss her Mum and siblings terribly. Jeff's former team mate at Dewsbury, Mick Stephenson would call to see Jeff and Sue as he was living and working out of Sydney and that made things a little easier. One or two of the players' wives would take Sue and Paul out for the day and drive for hours to get to their destination. 'Going out on these day trips made me realise just how big Australia is,' said Sue.

As sometimes happens, a few players and their wives saw Jeff as a threat and were not happy about the club bringing over British players. Cronulla, as a club, had always shown an interest in bringing over British players and, I may add, usually the good class internationals of this country. Tommy Bishop and Cliff Watson were heroes at Cronulla as was Roger Millward just before Jeff's arrival.

Besides being a good club, the idyllic surroundings of the area acted as a fantastic attraction with its beautiful beaches and surf. Who could say no to an invitation to play there? But Sue's friendly, outgoing nature soon won over any unhappy wives. Jeff loved the Australian way of life. He soon became used to the extra tough training regime and was ready for the challenge of the Australian competition. In his sixth game, against St George at Kogarah Oval, things were going well for Jeff in the playing stakes. He was becoming familiar with his team mates' style of play and they were warming to his enthusiastic running and tackling. Then, suddenly, Jeff was hit by a perfect hard (and fair) tackle around his legs from the side but found great difficulty in getting back to his feet. He didn't know it at the time but he had torn the cruciate ligament in his knee. In those days this was possibly the worst of the knee ligaments to damage and few players recovered to play on the injured knee again. Jeff didn't know this at the time. The procedure in Australia back then was to be taken to the treatment room near the dressing rooms where the club doctor would examine the extent of the injury and, in most cases, strap up the damaged joint. If the injury felt okay then the player would return to the field as soon as possible. This was not the case with Jeff as the injury was too bad. A temporary splint was placed on the leg and that was it for the day.

Jeff had a week of intense treatment at the club and trained on the injured leg, albeit at a restricted pace. He was selected to play the following weekend at home. Jeff recalls:

> What the club did in a case such as this was to send the injured player to see a specialist who strapped the injured leg and it felt great. I could bend the joint without pain and it was like being normal again. I went to the game and started as normal and after about 20 minutes, I took the ball up, hit the front on tackler and was okay, as I had been from the start of the game. A split second later another tackler hit my injured leg smack on the side of the knee joint and bingo, it creaked again and this time I knew it was bad.

An inspection of the injury at the local hospital proved that a reconstruction of the knee was required. This entailed a serious and fairly new type of surgery which had been developed in American Grid Iron football. The first job was to contact Dewsbury to explain the situation and ask for permission from the British club to perform the operation. This was obtained immediately. It was pioneering surgery at the time and, seemingly, a tendon was moved across and stapled into position to support the cruciate ligament to which it was fixed.

> The club were fantastic to me and Sue. I had played around 10 games for them and they wanted me to stay until I had recovered and was able to play again but that was months away. Sue was still feeling homesick, although not as bad as when we first arrived. We decided to come home so I could recover there. We thought that was the fairest thing to do for Dewsbury too. We informed Cronulla of our decision and they accepted this in good faith. They looked after us right up to us arriving back in Manchester, making sure we had seats with extra leg room as my injured leg was in a splint and un-bendable!

Playing in Australia was over for Jeff temporarily; although he would play in Australia again as a British Rugby League Lion on tour. In Jeff's mind gaining a place on a tour would be the icing on the cake for his successful rugby career.

Before Jeff agreed to go play for Cronulla, he contacted Mr Harry Womersley, who was on the RL selection committee, on a personal matter. Jeff wanted to find out if he, as a current Great Britain player, had a chance of making the 1977 World Cup team to play in the competition over in Australia. If he had then he would relinquish his chance of going to Cronulla. Mr Womersley told Jeff that he could not say for sure if he would gain selection but he would be surprised if he didn't. As we know Jeff considered a 'bird in the hand' to be a more assured situation so that is what he opted for. His desire to play for his country in Australia would have overcome his eventual destination of Cronulla had Mr Womersley been able to give him the nod about the forthcoming World Cup competition.

So it was back to Birstall for the long painful route back to fitness but he never expected to go through the trauma of another serious knee operation so soon after the experience of the Australian trip. Jeff waited patiently, did his physio and began jogging in straight lines but despite sweating buckets, he found bending his knee fully to be almost impossible, no matter how he tried. Because of the stiffness he found it restricted his pace and this meant he could not play until he had resolved the problem. The consultant at the local Batley hospital examined Jeff's injured leg and said that if the injury had have taken place in this country he would not have touched it and Jeff would have been left with a stiff leg for life. Jeff remembers:

Because of the new ideas being used in Australia, via America, I was given another 14 years of playing. If I had injured the leg in England it would have finished me. So I continued working hard at my physiotherapy, trying to bend the knee to enable me to run that bit faster. I was laid on my stomach in the hospital gym, trying to bend the knee when a nurse walked past and asked what I was doing. I told her and she said 'I will give you a hand' and pushed my knee towards my back with some force. I immediately had this searing pain across my knee and down the back of my leg. I knew something had gone awfully wrong as I was in real pain. Gradually the pain subsided but the knee was not at all right.

The consultant saw me quickly and an X-ray showed that the staples holding the tendon in place from the Australian surgery had sprung open thus allowing the tendon to be loose and not do its job. The consultant told me that the Australian doctor had 'Used a sledge hammer to crack a walnut!' He admitted me into hospital again and repaired the damage. Sue keeps those staples that were taken out of my leg in a glass file and they're big.

After the second operation I found that with some strong physio work I was able to bend the knee almost to pre injury level. Looking back to those days I can't stress enough just how much Cronulla looked after me whilst injured. After returning home I couldn't work for a few months and to give an idea of just how ill the injury made me, I lost over a stone in weight in about eight days. But the Aussie club gave me everything they said they would and they were brilliant to us.

Jeff's last appearance for Dewsbury before going to Australia was against Hull FC at The Boulevard on 24 April 1977. His first appearance back at Crown Flatt was against Castleford on 24 March 1978, exactly 11 months later. Dewsbury were lifted by Jeff's return and played exceptionally well to record a fine 23–5 win. Jeff missed the next game only three days later but was back for the tough game against Workington Town at Dewsbury in the 16 points all draw on 2nd April. He was at loose forward for the trip to Central Park, Wigan where Dewsbury suffered a 21–5 defeat. Jeff missed the final two league games against Featherstone Rovers home and Bradford Northern away because of fluid in his injured knee.

Jeff's experience in Australia plus his injury which kept him out of football and out of work for so long made him wonder how green was the grass over the hill. He had played in some cracking Dewsbury teams and won the championship with them but it struck him that being a one club man possibly was not the best for him. Jeff had ambitions to win medals at club level and to tour Australia with the Rugby League touring team. He desperately wanted to play at Wembley in a side who won regularly. This would mean he would step up to the payment level of his international team mates. He was a current international forward so why couldn't he cash in on that fact?

Jeff was now almost back to his top fitness. After returning to work as a brick drawer, his job of lifting and pulling heavy weights every day enhanced his training and he found that soon the power returned to his running and tackling. Word filtered down the grapevine that if he started the next season fit with no knee problems, St Helens and Leeds would be interested in signing him. This drove Jeff on in training and by 20 August 1978, Jeff was raring to go.

Castleford away was the first game of this season in the Yorkshire Cup and Jeff had a good game in the second row. Castleford had pace and skill in their backs with Terry Richardson and John Joyner forming a dangerous partnership on the right hand side and Gary Stephens a box of tricks at scrum half. Doncaster at Tatters Field was earmarked as the first league game of the season and Jeff was moved to loose forward as his pace and strength had returned in full. It was thought that his powers would be better used to give him more scope in loose play. The move paid off as Jeff had a blinder with breaks and well timed passes plus his devastating tackling and the two league points were taken with a score of 16–13.

Another away tie, two days after the Doncaster game in the BBC2 Floodlit Trophy, took Dewsbury to Lawkholme Lane, Keighley where the home side took their chances well to win 10–0. Five days later Dewsbury took on Blackpool Borough at Crown Flatt and won 14–9 in the league. About this time Jeff asked the Dewsbury committee to be placed, once again, on the transfer list. He considered that he had proved his fitness and also that his injured leg was fully healed and felt that the time was right for him to move for the sake of his career.

Although St Helens and Leeds were interested, a team nearer home made a move for him. Jeff received a phone call from Mr Harry Womersley, chairman of Bradford Northern, asking if Jeff would be interested in talking to him with a view to the Bradford club signing him. The chairman asked if he may call that evening to discuss Jeff's private terms and have a general talk about the club and its staff. Within the hour Mr Womersley and his fellow board associate Mr Windass were knocking on Jeff and Sue's door to speak to them. Jeff recalls, 'Both men made an impression on me and talked sensibly about the game and what they wanted for the club. Their coach, Peter Fox, had already had a successful career in coaching and was renowned for a style that involved big, tough forwards'.

The two Bradford directors told Jeff that Peter was interested in Jeff signing for the Odsal club. 'What are you looking for Jeff?' asked Mr Womersley.

Jeff remembers the conversation they had and how he made his decision to move:

> I think it would be more to the point if I asked you what you are prepared to offer me! I'm looking for a little financial security and appreciate there will be a great chance to earn good money playing with Bradford. It's the contractual side of the business I'm most concerned about.'
>
> Mr Womersley responded, 'We both appreciate you're concerned about securing a decent contract'. He went on to outline a good contract and asked how it sounded. It was the best offer I had ever had and it certainly would give Sue and Paul a good standard of living so I agreed. The speed that the two directors leaped out of their seats and rushed to shake hands on the deal made me wonder if I had answered too quickly! But that was me and how I reacted was a sign that I was satisfied totally with the offer. Dewsbury had given permission for them to speak to me, all that was to be done now was for the two clubs to strike a deal over the transfer details. I was asked not to mention this move until it was agreed by the two clubs and that I should keep on playing at Crown Flatt until the deal was completed. Mr Womersley said they wanted me at Odsal as soon as possible and things may happen quite quickly. So it was training as usual at Crown Flatt with the next game against Oldham at the

Watersheddings which the Lancastrians won 15–10.

There was no word from Bradford that week so I was still a Dewsbury player as the club entered the first round of the John Player Trophy at home against the amateur lads from Milford ARLFC, Leeds. Despite throwing everything at us Dewsbury proved just too quick and strong for them and we marched into round two with a 38–5 win. On 1 October 1978 I played my final game for Dewsbury at home to York. I had left Dewsbury once before to play out in Australia but I'd had the feeling that I would return to the club that had given me so many good times. This time it was so different as a transfer was involved making it almost impossible to return. The last team I played in at Dewsbury was, Brunyee; Agar, Lowe, Artis, Mitchell; Nigel Stephenson, Ferres; Weavill, Price, Hankins, Grayshon, Dave Woods and Welsh, the subs were, Richardson and Craven and we lost this game 12–6.

So I burnt my boats but I felt excited about the move. I was also joining a man, Peter Fox, who was to have a big involvement in the remainder of my career. In time Peter advised me to change positions from a mobile back rower to a ball handling open side prop forward. But Peter was more than that, he became a good friend and his knowledge of the game had a great effect on me. I reported to Odsal and signed the registration form for the club on Tuesday 3 October 1978.

5

FOX AND ODSAL

Jeff had played many times at Odsal both in league and international games. Despite this he was always surprised at the size of the dressing rooms at the top of the mountainous banking that formed the natural bowl of that wonderful ground. The ground, which holds the world Rugby League record for an attendance at a game of 102,575 at the replay of the 1954 drawn Wembley final between Warrington and Halifax, is still an awe inspiring place. So imagine the thoughts of Jeff as he stood looking down at that huge vista! Jeff knew all his new team mates as he had played against them for Dewsbury and England and with some of them for Yorkshire and in international football.

Jeff's first ever game for Bradford was one to remember as it was against the touring Australians. These tourists were big and strong. Back then the game in Australia was forming into the power it has today. A strong coaching set up combined with all things good in the game further enhanced players who made the top grade. Three of Jeff's former team mates from Cronulla made the touring party, Steve Rogers, Steve Keen and Greg Pierce. Possibly this game is remembered for the two tries and two goals scored by the great Neil Fox who was in the veteran stage of his magnificent career. Tony Fisher dropped a goal to give Bradford 11 points against the Australians' 21 points. But the size and ferocity of the Bradford pack on that day gives an indication of how this excellent Bradford side developed under the expert guidance of Peter Fox.

Despite the defeat Jeff was pleased with his Bradford debut and the *Telegraph & Argus,* Bradford's local evening newspaper gave glowing reports on his industrious work load. Within a few weeks Peter was involved in his wheeler-dealer style and incoming players to his already strong squad were the experienced and clever footballer Nigel Stephenson plus Steve Ferres from Dewsbury, the much travelled forward Geoff Clarkson, the great ball winning hooker Keith Bridges from Featherstone Rovers and the tough, Great Britain utility forward from Humberside, Len Casey. Peter released Johnny Wolford, Jack Austin and a little later Bob Haigh to Dewsbury. Len Casey and Jeff became great friends both on and off the field.

So would the change of club and the influence of Peter Fox give a boost to Jeff's career? Changing to a 'big' club can normally give an adrenalin rush to one's game and although that did occur with Jeff, he was now an experienced player and his strong, quiet persona allowed him to play his football in a controlled and professional manner. Playing alongside the superb Neil Fox regularly was another great boost to Jeff's play as, although playing in international and county football with some of the best players our game could muster, to play with a master footballer such as Neil each week gave Jeff experience of some sublime skills of the game.

Wigan always brought a buzz of excitement whenever they came to Odsal and it was another big day when, the week after the Australian game, Bradford entertained Wigan. Jeff had settled well and gave a performance at loose forward that eased away any doubts about his leg injury from Cronulla. He was in splendid form and the *Telegraph & Argus* star writer Brian Smith suggested: 'At last Northern have come up trumps in signing a top class back row forward in Jeff Grayshon. His display against Wigan was exceptional in each department'.

The following weekend Jeff was out of the side! That weekend Bradford Northern and York contested the Yorkshire County Cup final at Headingley and Jeff was cup-tied as he had played in the first round tie for Dewsbury at Castleford and therefore was forced out by the rules of the competition. Bob Haigh slotted in at loose forward for Jeff and Bob was a try scorer in Bradford's 18–8 win. Jeff recalls:

> Peter had bought well in strengthening the side and because so many good players were at the club we had to adhere to a rotation system. Now and again Peter would ease in a young player and whoever was left out that weekend would be told in good time beforehand.

Jeff returned for the game after the County Cup final when Northern travelled to Hull Kingston Rovers to take on the tough Robins at Craven Park. The result was a fine win for the Robins by 10–6 in a fearsome encounter. It was back to winning ways then with two grand wins against Leigh by 13–7 at Hilton Park, a game which saw Nigel Stephenson make debut at stand off half for Bradford. Then Bradford Northern took on Rochdale Hornets at Odsal, winning by 30–18. Jeff took a knock against Rochdale and the shrewd Peter Fox rested him for the trip to The Boulevard to take on Hull FC in the second round of the John Player Trophy. Bradford were successful, winning 18–12, and moved on to round three.

January 1979 brought an exciting air amongst the players as

the 1979 Rugby League touring squad was expected to be named. Word was out that because recent touring British players were injured and returning home with replacements sent out, the number of the touring squad would be increased from 26 to 30 players. The usual number of tourists, 26, was made up of two positions each. The extra four players would certainly add confidence against serious injuries plus it gave four extra players the chance of a lifetime.

Previously Jeff was quoted in the local newspaper, in a question and answer interview as to what his ambitions were in the professional game. He answered in truth, back then, when he said that he wanted to become a regular player for Dewsbury and hopefully play for Yorkshire. He had given this interview just after signing for Dewsbury so obviously after joining Bradford, his ambitions became that bit higher. Jeff always wanted the experience of playing at Wembley, as does every professional Rugby League player and then, after talking to team mates who had toured, he wanted selection for a full tour of Australia and New Zealand. History tells us that Jeff missed out on playing at Wembley and that was one of the great heartaches felt by those who know and respected his abilities as a player. He had, of course, played in Australia for Cronulla and his mates over there realised that his best was not shown because of the dreadful leg injury he had gained. But he battled on and hoped to win more medals at Odsal.

Bradford Northern beat Featherstone Rovers in the league at Post Office Road 18–7 and Wakefield Trinity took Bradford all the way before losing 16–13 at Odsal in the third round of the John Player Trophy. Then seven away games on the trot followed. The games were Huddersfield at Fartown won 28–10, Leeds at Headingley won 10–5, Widnes at Naughton Park lost 0–17, Workington Town at Derwent Park won 13–6, Widnes again at

Naughton Park in the semi final of the John Player lost 21–3, Barrow at Craven Park won 12–11 and Swinton in the Challenge Cup first round at Station Road, on 20th February, won 8–2. This was a vital time for Jeff and his ambitions to tour Australia and New Zealand. Not only were the crucial Challenge Cup ties forthcoming but the European Championships were due to start early in March and it was muted that the touring team would be selected immediately after the final game between England and France at Wilderspool, Warrington on 24th March, with the touring team flying out around 20th May.

It was around this time that the Rugby League Council dropped a bombshell by announcing that there would be a new Great Britain coach in charge for the tour. Peter Fox had had control of the Great Britain coaching job and had done as well as anyone since Johnny Whiteley led the successful 1970 tour with Frank Myler as his captain. The late Jim Challinor as coach, with Chris Hesketh as his captain, had gone within an ace of beating the Australians on the 1974 tour so much was expected, in the way of success, from the side going out in May. The bombshell was the news that Peter Fox would be replaced as coach by the excellent former Great Britain captain and current St Helens coach Eric Ashton. Peter was decimated by the news and the great dream of his to be the third brother of the Fox family to tour on an Australasian trip was gone! Jeff could well have lost an ally on the selection team but he had an ace up his sleeve with the fact that his club Chairman, Mr Harry Womersley was the tour manager. This meant Jeff had to keep up his club form, which was excellent, in order to gain selection for England in the vital European Championships and then play out of his skin in those games.

But back on the club scene Bradford went into the semi final of the John Player to face their old cup foes, Widnes at

Naughton Park. Confident they may have been, even after the defeat only seven days before in the league game against the 'Chemics' but Widnes lived up to their recent title of 'Cup Kings' and played well to beat Bradford out of sight 21–3. Into round two of the Challenge Cup went Bradford where they faced a tough, bruising encounter with the strong Hull Kingston Rovers at Odsal, gaining a cracking result for Northern in the shape of a 14–7 win. Then Jeff was informed by official letter that he was selected to play for England against Wales on 16th March at Naughton Park, Widnes.

The round three draw was kind to Bradford and saw them entertain Hull FC. Another titanic struggle took place as both teams knocked lumps off each other in an attempt to reach the semi final. This tremendous game ended at 8 points all with the replay at The Boulevard on Wednesday 14th March, just two days before the crucial Wales game. There was no question of crying off the cup tie. Jeff wanted Wembley badly and his loyalty to both Peter Fox and the Bradford club made his decision easy, he would play in the replay.

Jeff and Len Casey had scored Bradford's tries and Neil Fox had kicked one goal in the draw at Odsal and all three of these tough forwards knew that it would be even tougher over there on Humberside. It worked out exactly that way too as in a desperately hard and brutal game Bradford won through on guts and determination to an 8–4 memorable win. A big bonus was that Jeff, although having one of his best games for Bradford, was uninjured and fit for the international game.

England Versus Wales, European Championship, Naughton Park, Widnes, 16 March 1979

This season's European Championship was a three team affair involving England, Wales and France. The RFL decided not to include an Other Nationalities side as quite a few of the leading clubs refused to release their overseas stars. So the teams lined up at Widnes with more than this Championship to play for; a tour place was on the line.

There never has been a Wales v England game at Rugby League without that bit of biff and bash and this was no exception. As expected big Jim Mills and almost as big Harry Beverley had things to say to each other and to be fair the tough Harry Beverley came off worse for wear but he had given almost as much back and the mutual respect of both players remains to this day. Jeff did his chances of a tour place a great deal of good with a non stop performance particularly in his tackling of the tough Welsh pack. Wales were level pegging at half time with a score of 5 points all after Harold Box had come into the three quarter line to slide over and convert. Box landed another goal in the second half to give Wales 7 points but the second half belonged to England and the home nation pulled away with tries by Keith Mumby, Keith Smith and substitute John Woods, on for Gary Stevens. Woods landed two second half goals to go with Mumby's one goal to give the England team a winning margin of 15–7. Dave Watkinson had replaced the battle scarred Harry Beverley and Mike Nicholas was used in place of Tommy Cunningham. Later, Paul Prenderville was introduced in place of Nicholas.

Jeff was optimistic about his chances of selection to tour after he had given himself every chance in this game against Wales. The league fixture with Featherstone Rovers on Sunday 25th March at Post Office Road was a crucial one as Bradford were in prime place to finish top of the league if they played up to form. Jeff was selected to play against France at Wilderspool Stadium, Warrington on the 24th and was pleased that Peter pencilled him in as a substitute to play the day after at Featherstone.

England Versus France, European Championship, Wilderspool, Warrington, 24 March 1979

In the game against France several changes were made from the side which won against Wales. This meant more prospective tourists were given a chance to display their wares in front of the tour selectors. France came to this match in a determined mood. They had beaten Wales in the first game of the series 15–8 and were confident they could win this competition with a victory against England. But the home side started well and by half time had forced a 12–2 lead. Both Eric Hughes and Tommy Martyn showed good pace in scoring tries and John Woods kicked three goals against the one penalty goal kicked by A. Touchagues. The only scores in the second half were the two further goals by Touchagues to give the final score of England 12 France 6. The winning trophy was returned to the safe keeping of the Rugby Football League in Leeds and although the purists moaned about the closeness of the result, the win for England was never in doubt.

The nervous waiting began as the touring team had been selected and all that was left was to notify those chosen about the requirements of the tour. On Wednesday morning the letter arrived telling Jeff that another dream of his had been fulfilled as he was selected for the trip of a lifetime. Despite the great news of the tour, life went on as usual. With one eye on the crucial game after the Featherstone trip, that of Widnes in the semi final of the Challenge cup to be played at Swinton, the Bradford team found Featherstone Rovers in defiant mood and they produced a strong performance against a Northern side with a shade of the semi final on their minds! The Rovers won 25–11.

On then to the most important cup game of the season at Station Road. Peter Fox's strategy must have been to play a side at the start of the game which was quite capable of beating Widnes but his ace up his sleeve was his strength on the bench where the excellent Peter Roe and the great Neil Fox were awaiting the call to action. Bradford's starting side included Mumby; Barends, Gant, Parker, David Redfearn; Stephenson, Alan Redfearn; Ian Van Bellen, Dyson, Thompson, Jeff, Trotter and Casey. Despite the big experienced pack Peter selected, Widnes won the lion's share of possession from the set scrums and this was possibly why Widnes won the game and went on to beat Wakefield Trinity in the final at Wembley. This was a crushing blow for Jeff even accepting the great season he had experienced at Odsal. Looking back there was so little between the teams in that semi final, with the score of Widnes 14 Bradford Northern 11, that the game could have been won and Jeff's ambition of playing in a Wembley final achieved. But the gods smiled upon the Widnes side and allowed them through. Widnes won the game fair and square and when one remembers their multi talented squad it is easy to see why. With players of the calibre of Dave Eckersley, Stuart Wright, Mick George, Eric Hughes, Reg Bowden, Jim Mills, Glyn Shaw, Mick Adams and Doug Laughton in their ranks they were as good as anything in the league. Three days after the semi final defeat Salford were the visitors to Odsal in the league game and surprisingly beat Northern by 12–8.

A glance at the number of games played by Jeff for Bradford since his debut against the Aussies on 8 October 1978 tells of his determination, fitness and durability. Of the possible 36 games remaining in that season after the Australian game, Jeff was involved in 31 including two games as substitute. This was a glowing record for a player who triumphed over his serious leg injury only a half a season before.

A trio of stiff away games followed the Salford defeat. Rochdale Hornets and Wakefield Trinity were both beaten 16–8 and 8–6 respectively but Castleford threw a spanner in the works by beating Northern at Wheldon Road 28–12. Peter Fox had scrutinized the remaining fixtures and the dates of the matches left to play. Bradford obviously wanted to end the league programme in as high a place as possible to give themselves as much advantage as they could in the premiership play offs. But no wonder Peter looked at the dates of the games to be played as Warrington surprised everyone by winning at Odsal 22–14 on 18th April only three days after the defeat by Castleford. There followed a big win against Wakefield Trinity at Odsal 50–5, Jeff charging over for Bradford's final try.

In these days of players complaining of too many matches too close together, it is interesting to look at the dates of games at the run in at the season's end. Of course an eye had to be kept on the season's end as the 1979 tour of Australia had to leave around 20th May for the Southern Hemisphere. Bradford had to play Wakefield Trinity who were beaten by 50 points on 27th April, on the 29th St Helens came to Odsal and won 13–12, the day after, the 30th, Bradford were beaten at St Helens 31–15. The day after that, 1st May, Bradford beat Workington Town at Odsal 16–3 and two days later, on 3rd May Bradford played Wigan at Central Park and were beaten 23–3. Still the games came thick and fast. A home win over Huddersfield on 8th May by 38–8 was followed by another game at Odsal on 10 May against Hull Kingston Rovers which again resulted in a win (26–4) for Bradford.

The final league game of the season was played on 12th May against Widnes at Odsal and the Chemics recorded a fine 27–19 win.

These results left Bradford with a tough play off game against Hull Kingston Rovers at Craven Park. It was another blood and guts affair with some great football and some vigorous tackling. There were dust ups all over the pitch but in between the fighting came some excellent tries and plays. Bradford triumphed 18–17 and the victory was down to the superb work of their pack which on the day comprised Ian Van Bellen, Keith Bridges, Jimmy Thompson, Jeff Grayshon, George Mordue and Len Casey and the two forward subs, Dennis Trotter and Colin Forsyth.

This great win was followed in the semi final by a wonderful display again by exactly the same Bradford forwards who had done so well at Hull Kingston Rovers. The result at Widerspool was another win for this grand Bradford side by 14–11. Bradford now faced Leeds in the premiership final at Fartown, Huddersfield on 27th May. Seven players were involved in the final who then had to follow the main party to Australia immediately afterwards. The tour coach, Eric Ashton, would travel with the last team members David Barends, Jeff Grayshon, Len Casey, Alan Redfearn and Keith Mumby of Bradford and David Ward and John Holmes of Leeds.

Bradford Northern Versus Leeds, Premiership Final, Fartown, Huddersfield, 27 May 1979

The final was a one sided affair and as Jeff said:

Leeds were running hot from the first whistle. We were always a little slow to start and Leeds took advantage to produce a great performance. We were beaten by 24–2. We never looked like getting to grips with them. In the end Leeds were worthy winners and lifted the trophy.

Leeds blasted away the Northern challenge with tries from Alan Smith, David Smith and David Ward and seven goals and a drop goal from Kevin Dick answered only by a Steve Ferres penalty goal.

6

RETURN TO OZ

So the time had come to join the other already Australia based tourists. Jeff said a sweetest goodbye to Sue and joined the other players at Odsal to drive to Manchester airport for the Qantas flight to Sydney for the three month tour. The jumbo jet travelled via Amsterdam, Athens, Bahrain, Bangkok, Singapore and on to Sydney. Eight tired tourists disembarked from that Qantas aircraft in Sydney to board yet another smaller aircraft to fly up the coast to link with the main body of players who were, by this time, up in Wide Bay, North Queensland. The tourists had played two games already, against North Queensland, won 24–5 and Central Queensland, won 20–11. The original touring party consisted of Mick Adams [Widnes], David Barends [Bradford Northern], Len Casey [Bradford Northern], Steve Evans [Featherstone Rovers], Peter Glynn [St Helens], Jeff Grayshon [Bradford Northern], Phil Hogan [Hull Kingston Rovers], John Holmes [Leeds], Eric Hughes [Widnes], Mel James [St Helens], John Joyner [Castleford], Doug Laughton [Widnes], Graham Liptrot [St Helens], Brian Lockwood [Hull Kingston Rovers], Tommy Martyn [Warrington], Roy Mathias [St Helens], Jim Mills [Widnes], Roger Millward [Hull Kingston Rovers], Keith Mumby [Bradford Northern], Steve Nash [Salford], George Nicholls [St

Helens], Steve Norton [Hull FC], Alan Redfearn [Bradford Northern], Trevor Skerrett [Wakefield Trinity], Mike Smith [Hull Kingston Rovers], Gary Stephens [Castleford], Charlie Stone [Hull FC], David Ward [Leeds], David Watkinson [Hull Kingston Rovers] and John Woods [Leigh]. Unfortunately three players had to return home injured early in the tour and the replacements sent out from Britain included John Burke [Wakefield Trinity] for Jim Mills, George Fairbairn [Wigan] for Tommy Martyn and Dave Topliss [Wakefield Trinity].

Eric Ashton decided to give the newly arrived players time to acclimatise to their surroundings and would not play all the newcomers together in their first run out in a game. The hotel was a quaint building, a bit like a hotel in a western movie. The first problem that faced Jeff and his room mate Len Casey was the box like room in which these two big men had been allocated. Jeff recalls:

Len and I were shown our room and when both of us were in it together plus our touring baggage, we had no space at all. Len and I looked at each other bemused before finding Eric Ashton to explain the problem. Eric had a look at the room with us and after seeing the size of it he immediately contacted the hotel manager and we were soon given a room plenty big enough for Len and me.

The training each day was light and varied. Our physio from Bradford, Ronnie Barritt, and Eric took us out for the daily stints and as all the squad had so recently ended a tough season there were no punishing routines. We were as fit as we could ever be with our season just ended so the training programme involved team bonding exercises to unite the squad. Very quickly that bond was formed between every member of the squad and, as usually happens on tour, we looked after each other particularly on the field of play. Eric wanted it that way as his experience told him that only a totally united team effort would allow us to beat the Aussies in Test football. He also knew that all the best preparations in the world could be blown away if the Aussies went into overdrive and they had the bounce of the ball. These things Eric, or any coach, could not foresee. But we all suddenly settled in and for those of us on our first tour, touring life—so different to anything we had ever experienced before—became really good fun, except for the constant packing and unpacking as we moved further down the eastern seaboard of Australia.

To be fair to the Australians, they looked after us as though we were kings. Invitations to dinner, personal appearances at various league clubs, meals out with sponsors all slotted into this touring life and there were few evenings when we were without some place to visit as a team. Our weekly allowance was $105 each. This was to cover any personal requirements we might have. Food was the biggest outlay from our allowance but we soon realised that we were fed every evening so the $105 helped us considerably with all the out of pocket needs that arose.

Although all the players took the training periods seriously, the feeling was of being relaxed yet focused on the tour. Some of the games organised by the Australian Rugby League were against teams who were renowned tough customers and in previous tours the Lions lost quite a few. Jeff and Alan Redfearn were selected to play their first games on 2nd June against North Coast at the beautiful resort of Tweed Heads. Both Jeff and Alan were to be substitutes. Tweed Heads is on the border between Queensland and New South Wales, just south of Surfers Paradise and Coolangatta. The result of this tough game was a resounding 33–6 win for the tourists. Both Jeff and Alan were given an extended run and both performed well and Eric Ashton was pleased that six of the tourists' seven tries were scored by his backs. Steve Evans 2, Roy Mathias 2, Phil Hogan 2 and Trevor Skerrett registered tries and John Woods landed six goals.

Three days later a Lions team flew down into New South Wales to take on Northern Division whilst the remainder of the squad returned to Brisbane. The team against Northern

Division, played at Tamworth, met with fierce opposition and Jeff was selected in the second row. Jeff's team mate at loose forward was his room mate Len Casey. The Aussies had a simple game plan, to knock the stuffing out of the tourists in any way they chose. The players had to watch their backs as off the ball hits and late tackles fell like rain on the Lions. A number of fights broke out, mainly as the tourists defended themselves and the referee let almost anything go. The tourists won through in the end 20–11 as Keith Mumby, David Barends and Peter Glynn scored tries, John Woods kicked another five goals and Mick Adams landed a drop goal.

The team that played at Tamworth rejoined the full squad back up in Brisbane as two days after the Northern Division game there was a real banana skin of a game against Queensland in Brisbane. Most people know of the highly competitive nature of Queenslanders, especially when in opposition against Great Britain and, of course, in the fierce State of Origin matches, so remembering previous brutal encounters in tourist games a team was selected to match the Northern State if the game went the biff way. Jeff was rested as he had played in the two matches before. True to form this game was a hard slog from the first whistle. The tough Queenslanders took no prisoners as they crashed into the Brits lifted by the ultra partisan spectators cheering every crunching home tackle. The result was a 25–19 win for the Lions.

Training stepped up a few gears as the first Test in Brisbane approached. More tactical application was introduced as Eric Ashton worked out his game plan for the crucial game on the Lang Park ground. But before that first Test the squad packed up their gear again and travelled due west, inland 100 miles, to Toowoomba to take on possibly the hardest of the district teams. Toowoomba did exactly what they had done to several touring teams, they beat the Lions 19–16 on a hot, sultry afternoon. Jeff was one of three substitutes on the bench for this game but when he got his chance on the pitch he gave it a good shot and in fact, according to the local newspaper coverage of the game, was one of the Lions successes in the pack.

Lions Versus Australia, First Test, Lang Park, Brisbane, 16 June 1979

The team flew back to Brisbane to link up with the whole squad. They had six days to recover from the Toowoomba game and prepare to take on Australia. Jeff met up with some of his former team mates at Cronulla as the tension mounted towards the weekend. This was the first ever Test match to be played under floodlights in Australia.

Despite his performance off the bench Jeff wasn't in the team selected for the first Test. Unfortunately on the day Great Britain were never in the hunt! Playing against a non existent defence the Australians dominated the game from the start. Unfortunately the Lions were on the end of a 35–0 hiding. Trevor Skerrett was sent off for using his elbow to stop Alan McMahon, Mick Cronin kicked 10 goals, Kerry Boustead and Ray Price scored two tries apiece and Larry Corowa crossed for another try. As the Rugby League historian Robert Gate mentions in *Rugby League Lions*, 'this was the biggest loss in a Test match in Australia and the first time the tourists were nilled. It was an unmitigated disaster, Great Britain had hit rock bottom'. The Aussie press went to town verbally attacking various British players. To say Eric Ashton was disappointed would be an understatement. His main job was to lift the players back into positive thinking. The dismissal of Trevor Skerrett had little bearing on the outcome of this Test but another worry for coach Eric Ashton was the injury list of his players. The big injury was to tour captain Doug Laughton who aggravated a knee problem and in fact played only one more game on this tour. The injury list left Eric Ashton with only 16 players fit for the next game against Brisbane again at Lang Park three days after the first Test.

Brisbane, led by one of the world's best players, Wally Lewis, had beaten the previous two touring teams and were a strong and aggressive side. Despite the injury crisis the Lions looked a good team on paper. For this match, played in driving rain throughout, the Lions team consisted of Keith Mumby; David Barends, Steve Evans, Eric Hughes, Peter Glynn; John Holmes, Alan Redfearn; Mel James, Graham Liptrot, Charlie Stone, Jeff Grayshon, Tommy Martyn and Len Casey. Subs: Roy Mathias and Trevor Skerrett. The Lions looked much sharper in the early stages of this game than in the whole of the first Test. Brisbane came at the Lions and took the lead with a penalty goal from John Barber but John Holmes levelled the scores just before half time. At the start of the second half Alan Redfearn took control and with good support from Len Casey and Jeff, the Lions again took hold of the game when David Barends scored a good try beating two Australians on the way to the line. Peter Glynn put up a high kick into the pouring rain and Tommy Martyn collected the ball to score a try converted by John Homes. As usually happened in these games, a flare up occurred between Len Casey and Wally Lewis with one or two other players joining in.

Brisbane's revival came in the final 15 minutes as Chris Close powered in for a strong try with Barber converting to take the score to the Lions 10 Brisbane 7. That's how the game finished despite great pressure on the Brits' try line by Brisbane. Britain had pulled back some respectability but the Aussie press still slaughtered them. More bad news for the tourists was that key back rower Tommy Martyn dislocated his shoulder late in the Brisbane game, one that had already undergone a reconstruction. The injury situation was becoming desperate and as Roger Millward and Tommy Martyn left the tour to go home for treatment they were replaced by David Topliss and George Fairbairn. Shortly after Jim Mills retired injured, replaced by John Burke.

Another poor display followed as the Lions took on Southern Division at Campbelltown. Jeff was one of the substitutes and again did as well as anyone but the Lions struggled to regain the good form they showed early in the tour. This game ended at 10 points all in what a top Rugby League writer called 'another drab performance'. The tourists needed a couple of good wins to regain their confidence but the tough games were now building up. The next game was a traditionally hard fixture against Newcastle. The area was notoriously brutal and composed of coal mines and tough players. Jeff was in the second row with Mick Adams as his partner. The Newcastle forwards played up to their hard reputation and the Lions pack met them blow for blow. Whilst the forwards were battling for supremacy the British backs made the most of the wide open spaces and the Lions try scorers were David Barends, Eric Hughes, John Joyner, Peter Glynn and Gary Stephens. The surprise goal kicker, Mick Adams, landed five goals in this 25–12 win for the tourists. Jeff deservedly picked up the man of the match award, a clock radio, for his massive tackling stint and his willing running wide out.

Games were regularly being played two or three days apart and the squad had the odd day relaxing away from the pressures of football. Sightseeing made for a good laugh and great comradeship amongst the players but the thought of levelling up the series was never far from their minds. The second vital Test at the Sydney Cricket Ground was now only one game away, that of the Riverina District at Wagga Wagga in the beautiful, lush inland farming area near the capital city of Canberra. The tour took the players to venues that were vast distances apart. Jeff sat out the Riverina game as Eric Ashton told him he would be on duty four days later in the second Test.

Lions Versus Australia, Second Test, Sydney Cricket Ground, 30 June 1979

Australia, rightfully so, selected an unchanged side for this Test in Sydney. Great Britain on the other hand made five changes in an effort to bring the series back to life after the hammering they received in the first Test. Newly arrived George Fairbairn was at full back as the Lions lined up. Again the Australians demonstrated their superiority with a blistering start, rattling up a 17–4 lead by half time. But the Lions began a come back early in the second half. John Joyner raced over after brilliant work by Gary Stephens, John Holmes, Len Casey and George Nicholls to cover half the length of the field. Then Eric Hughes kicked ahead twice in a run of 80 yards to register another Lions try and, with Woods converting both tries, the Lions pulled back to within three points of the Aussies. Jeff had tackled well, his work rate was outstanding and it was unfortunate that he should be involved along with Mick Adams in a slip up in defence when the Australian second row forward Rod Reddy gained possession of the ball 30 yards out from the Lions try line. No problems but, inexplicably, both Jeff and Mick were wrong footed by the nimble Aussie and he sprinted to the line for a fine try. Mick Cronin added two further goals and the reply was another penalty goal by John Woods but the Aussies had won the Ashes Cup by 24–16 and also the series.

Even the Aussie press relented a little by admitting that this was a far better performance by the Lions but the whole reason for the tour, which was to win the Ashes Cup, had failed in its efforts and the feeling in the Lions camp was one of total disappointment. Jeff himself, to this day, holds his hands up regarding that missed tackle on Rod Reddy:

> I had nailed him several times in this Test and had got to him in each case before he had hit his stride. Both Mick Adams and I seemed to have him covered then, like lightning, he stepped between us and left us standing. Afterwards I had a little thing about that miss and could only say that Rod beat both Mick and I fair and square. He was there, then away in a split second and I know for a fact that he has done the same to a lot of great tacklers in his career.

At the end of this game as the players walked into the tunnel to the dressing rooms, an Aussie player made a comment to the British team members causing George Nicholls to answer him back and offer a challenge to the Aussie forward. But officials rushed between the two big men and a fracas was avoided. It was accepted that it would have taken a brave man to withstand a challenge from George Nicholls.

But there was no time to sit around feeling sorry for themselves. Two days after the second Test the Lions had to face up to another tough traditional 'banana skin' of a game, against the district that had produced its share of Test players, that of Illawarra down in Wollongong. In Aboriginal language Wollongong means 'Where the land falls into the sea' and needless to say one or two touring teams had metaphorically fallen into the sea there.

Illawarra set about the tourists as they did in every tour

game they played in. High tackles came in from every direction and the Lions had to be watchful as three and four tacklers piled in with fists, elbows and knees at every opportunity. Naturally the Brits defended themselves and, in most cases, gave back more than they took. Great Britain could not shake off this tough and enthusiastic side and each time the Brits scored so did Illawarra. Of course it meant so much to these district sides if they managed to beat a touring team and, usually, a victory was posted throughout the district and talked about for years to come. This young Illawarra side certainly tried its best and besides knocking the tourists about a bit actually played some good football to notch up 13 points. The Lions scored four beautifully crafted tries through Roy Mathias, Steve Evans, Peter Glynn and Jeff Grayshon. Jeff's try was a forwards specialty as four of the tourist pack inter passed and Jeff took the final pass to race in for a fine try. George Fairbairn landed four goals to give the Lions their 18 points but it was a close run thing at the end. True to the Illawarra tradition the tourists had a shock at the tough way they were handled.

The next game for the tourists involved 150 miles of travel, to the westward side of the Blue Mountains, to take on Western Districts out in Orange, the next town to the west past Bathurst. The divisional side again put up a defiant display but the Lions went on to win 19–12. Eric Ashton swapped his team around for this game giving his key players a rest before the so called fourth 'Test match' against New South Wales in Sydney which was three days after the game at Orange.

The New South Wales team was usually made up of most of Australia's full Test team with just a couple of changes. Usually the new players brought into the team were full international players so the State team was not generally weakened in any

Jeff supports Nigel Stephenson with Terry Day watching as Les Dyl of Leeds covers in the 1972–73 Championship Final win at Odsal

Jeff shows his style and breaks clear covered by Leeds wingman Alan Smith in the 1972–73 Championship Final at Odsal

Dewsbury's second row partnership, John Bates and Jeff, receive their County Cap and badge from Dewsbury Vice Chairman Mr Roy Harter

Jeff passes to team mate John Clarke for Dewsbury at Station Road, Swinton with Joe Whittington in support

Great Britain 1979 Touring Squad at a photo call at Headingley,
Jeff is 4th from right, middle row

Des Drummond (centre) and Jeff accept their player of the
season awards from Keith Maklin (second left)

Jeff shows his
class for Bradford
Northern with
this break against
Barrow with
Keith Mumby in
support

Bradford V Widnes. Jeff held in the tackle by Mick Adams

Jeff at Odsal wondering, 'Why did the referee penalise me?'

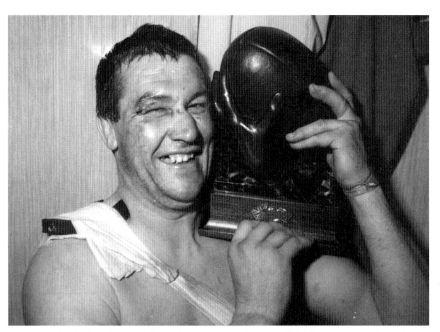

Jeff in the Elland Road dressing room with the Whitbread Trophy after the drawn series against New Zealand in 1985

The Great Britain side which won the French Presidents
Bowl in Limoux, June 1985. The author is holding the
bowl and Jeff is 4th from right, back row

Playing for Leeds, Jeff releases another perfect pass

Jeff, 36 years, is vaulted by Shaun Edwards, 17 years, as they prepare for the third Test against New Zealand at Elland Road. They were, at that time, the oldest and youngest ever to play for Great Britain

Jeff, a master ball handler, displays his skills for Featherstone Rovers watched by Kiwi team mate Trevor Clark

Jeff and son Paul after they had played directly against one another at open side prop in the Featherstone Rovers V Bradford Northern game. Sue told Paul, 'Don't hurt your dad'

Jeff (behind) and Mark Knapper make a sandwich of
the Keighley player in the game at Featherstone

Jeff protects himself
as he rides a tackle
against Widnes at
Post Office Road,
Featherstone

Great handling by Jeff as his perfect delivery is
watched by team mate Deryck Fox

Jeff concentrates as he is about to
enter the field from the subs
bench for Featherstone Rovers
© RLphotos.com

Sue and Jeff at Buckingham
Palace after Jeff received his
MBE from Her Majesty
Queen Elizabeth

way. The recent district games and now this tough State fixture had proved to be a difficult section of the tour. Strange as it seemed this 1979 Lions touring squad had beaten the usual tough sides who had proved so difficult to beat in earlier tours. But now they were facing this New South Wales outfit which was considered a 'shadow' Test team. The Australian Test selectors had withdrawn almost the whole side to give them a rest before the third and final Test only 14 days away.

Nevertheless the State team was still a strong side. It included four players who had international experience and the remainder were from good clubs in the Sydney league. It would be a severe test for a Lions side lacking in confidence in this key game against a team hell bent on making a name for itself. Some of the newer players hoped it would put them in the frame for future selection in the Test arena. Eric Ashton's depleted squad, still decimated by injuries, was selected to do a job in this game in which a good result would ensure the Australian public turned out for the final Test.

The team to play New South Wales at the Cricket Ground included George Fairbairn; Eric Hughes, John Joyner, John Woods, Roy Mathias; David Topliss, Alan Redfearn: Trevor Skerrett, David Watkinson, George Nicholls, Jeff Grayshon, Phil Hogan and Mick Adams. The subs were Steve Evans and David Ward. It was a different Great Britain side that the Aussie supporters saw at the Cricket Ground. The Brit's pack led by Trevor Skerrett and Jeff Grayshon got to grips with the big Aussie forwards. With George Nicholls and David Watkinson blocking any plays around the play the ball, Phil Hogan running with power wide out and Mick Adams showing all his craft to bring on Jeff and Trevor Skerrett into the gaps, there were some very surprised Aussies in the crowd. Steve Evans raced over for two tries, John Woods used his silky skills to great effect to register a fine try and George Fairbairn showed remarkable strength to force his way over for a try. John Woods kicked three goals and George Fairbairn dropped a superb goal to claim the 19–17 win for the tourists. Although the New South Wales side was not as strong as expected because the Aussie selectors vetoed the use of Test players in the current series, no one could take it away from the Lions that this was one of the best performances of the whole tour.

The final non Test match of the tour in Australia was against Monaro District in a game played at Queanbeyan, just south east of Canberra. In another hard, testing fixture the Lions won the contest 21–7. This was the final game of the tour for Jim Mills who had managed only five appearances because of an ongoing knee injury sustained in the win against Wide Bay in only the third game of the tour. The focus now was turned onto the last game of the Tour against Australia in the final Test in Sydney. The squad had relished the six day respite from the stresses of games and come the day of that final Test match were in a good and relaxed state of mind.

Lions Versus Australia, Third Test, Sydney Cricket Ground, 14 July 1979

The expected surge of interest in the Tour because of the Lions good win against New South Wales did not materialise and on the day of the game at the Cricket Ground only 16,854 spectators turned out for the final Test. This was a record low for a Test match in Australia. Australia selected a tried and tested side and had a confident look about them, like a team with nothing to lose. Reports of the game suggest that the Lions were determined to gain revenge for the two previous lost Test matches. Under extreme provocation, the reports said, the Australians maintained their composure and, more importantly, their discipline. The penalty count at the end of the game was 20–11 in the Aussies favour.

Even in the face of the tourists' aggression the Australians maintained their game plan and, despite one huge brawl and no doubt helped by Steve Norton being sent off in the second half, won the game at a canter. Reports say that 'the Lions were incapable of troubling Australia who won as they pleased. Britain's niggling tactics did not work against this well drilled Australian side'. Aussie tries came from Graham Eadie, Ray Price, Rod Reddy and Les Boyd with Mick Cronin landing eight goals. The Lions reply was a solitary John Woods penalty goal. So with a final score of 28–2, Australia ruled supreme with a 3–0 Ashes win.

* * * * *

On 15th July the 1979 British Lions Rugby League touring side packed their bags for the umpteenth time, not to travel the long ranges into the interior or up and down the long coastline, but to board a jet airplane and cross the Tasman Sea to the Island of the Long White Cloud, New Zealand. The first game in New Zealand was way up at the Northern end of the North Island at Whangarei to play one of the hardest matches in the whole itinerary of this tour, that of the New Zealand Maori. The Maori took the international games against any British touring side into the realms of warfare for 80 minutes. This Maori team was a big, athletic outfit and with the first Test match only four days later, the local lads were given the task of making life difficult for the tourists.

The cagey Eric Ashton guessed what would happen and played only four of his First Test side against the Maori. The Lions still packed a punch though and included Keith Mumby, David Barends, John Homes and David Watkinson in the side.

Jeff wasn't selected being one of the players kept back by Ashton for the Test. Graham Liptrot, Mel James and David Barends scored tries and Mick Adams landed three goals for the Lions in a very hard fought, no holds barred game. Jeff recalls, 'It never stopped raining from us landing in Auckland on arriving in New Zealand, to leaving 27 days later! We trained in the rain, went sight seeing in the rain, played our games in the rain and did everything in the bloody rain'. It poured down on first Test day and the pitch at Carlaw Park, Auckland was very heavy indeed.

Lions Versus New Zealand, First Test, Carlaw Park, Auckland, 21 July 1979

New Zealand selected a number of new faces for this game and most of them ended up moving across the world to play for British clubs. It was a time of great change in New Zealand's Rugby League with the tactical coaching of the great Ces Mountford, of Wigan fame as a player, then to be followed by another excellent coach, Graham Lowe. These two coaches suddenly made the Kiwis arguably the best international side of that era. Although winning this first Test match by 16–8and being control in open play, the Lions lost the scrums 12 to 4 but this was intentional as had they won the set pieces then they suspected that referee Mr Percival would murder them with penalty kicks just to keep the Kiwis in the game.

The Lions first try was a beautifully constructed piece of football as Phil Hogan had Eric Hughes racing clear inside his own 25 with a superb long pass. Hughes swept around Warren Collicoat and when being overhauled by the covering Dane O'Hara, turned the ball inside to the supporting Mike Smith who scorched the final 35 yards to the posts. The try was converted by George Fairbairn. Dick Uluave replied with a fine

New Zealand try after chasing a kick through by Collicoat. Steve Evans, Fairbairn and Hughes added further tries for the Lions and Fairbairn landed one goal to give Great Britain their 16 points. Fed Ah Kuoi added to the Kiwi total with a well taken try to give the home side their eight points. The exodus of New Zealand players over to the UK not long after saw O'Hara, Leuluai and Ah Kuoi serve at the Boulevard for Hull FC, Mark Broadhurst and Gordon Smith play for Hull Kingston Rovers, Graham West and Howie Tamati play at Central Park, Wigan and Kurt Sorenson, who played in the second Test, and Kevin Tamati went on to serve at Widnes.

It was still raining for the tourists' next fixture at the rural town of Huntly, north of the city of Hamilton where they were to play Northern District. Only Steve Evans, Alan Redfearn and Brian Lockwood were selected from the first Test squad but the team gave a splendid performance in beating the local district side 58–5. Further South now the Lions rested in the superb and picturesque district of Taranaki. The game against Central District was played in the lovely town of New Plymouth on the edge of the Taranaki National Park. Traditionally this was always a tough fixture as the Taranaki area had a tradition of producing tough forwards and equally tough backs. Jeff was included in a strong team and remembers, 'the word was that they always tested you out early. The big, strong Maori boys always played that way so you could expect the odd punch or elbow up in the tackle. They were not a dirty side, just rough and ready and if you stood your ground and gave a bit back then they warmed to you and things settled down'. They were rough and ready alright, determined to make the Lions remember the visit to New Plymouth. The heavy conditions tended to make it a forward battle anyhow so the players were prepared for any emergency. The result was a hard run out for the tourists which ended in a 14–5 victory for the Lions. Eric Hughes, Roy Mathias, Mike Smith and Gary Stephens scored the Lions tries and George Fairbairn landed one goal.

One more game before the second Test took the Lions to 'Windy' Wellington to take on the strong local Wellington area team. Jeff's three mates from Bradford Northern, David Barends, Alan Redfearn and Len Casey, all played in this game. Although the tackling was tough, the Lions managed to score seven tries with John Woods kicking nine goals. The score indicated a respectable 39–3 win. Now the tourists were faced by the short but usually hairy flight across the Cook Straights to the gloriously scenic South Island of New Zealand. The flights whilst in the South Island were, in the days of this tour, taken in light aircraft and the turbulence on these flights was legendary amongst the previous Lions teams. Jeff said, 'There were some upset tummies whilst travelling in the South Island with aircraft thrown all over the place. Ronnie Barritt loved it as he was a registered pilot but he was the only one of the party who did!'

Lions Versus New Zealand, Second Test, Addington Show Ground, Christchurch, 5 August 1979

The second Test was played at Christchurch, again in the rain, at the Addington Show Ground and once again the pitch was quite heavy. With only four games left on this tour it would have been easy for a bit of complacency to set in but Eric Ashton managed the troops wonderfully in an effort to keep the boilers stoked up. The referee, Mr Percival, decided that winning the scrums was not enough for the Kiwis and gave a rather ridiculous amount of penalties in favour of New Zealand to the tune of 19–8. But the Lions overcame this and Len Casey and Jeff had a great day together in the Lions second row, the tourists secured the series win by recording a 22–7 victory in this Test match. Try scorers for the Lions were Steve Evans, Eric Hughes, Len Casey and Jeff Grayshon with George Fairbairn landing five goals. For the Kiwis, Olsen Filipaino scored a thundering try and kicked two goals.

The final game in the South Island was across country from Christchurch on the East coast at the quaint town of Greymouth. This area is a stretch of the coastline battered by the Tasman Sea and the great rolling surf thundering up from Antarctica. The wide open terrain facing the huge waves was scary enough but the journey across the South Island from East coast to West coast was horrendous in the light airplane in which the tourists flew. Buffeted around, hitting pockets of air that sent the plane up or down in sudden bursts, battling head winds and in fact hitting every kind of weather in the 100 mile trip. The Lions were happy indeed to step down from that frightening experience. The West Coast district team was made up mostly of coal miners as that area was, at one time, the main coal producing site in the whole of New Zealand. The players from the West Coast were a tough breed of men, like the miners of our own coal mining areas of Wales, Cumberland and the Yorkshire and Lancashire coal fields. The result went the Lions way again 19–nil but it was a good hard game of Rugby League. The tourists went back across to Christchurch then embarked on the 450 mile flight up country to Auckland for the final two games of this tour. The next game was against New Zealand in the final Test, played at Carlaw Park in the mud.

Lions Versus New Zealand, Third Test, Carlaw Park, Aukland, 11 August 1979

The Kiwis had lost the series but this made them even more dangerous and the atrocious playing conditions made the Third Test certain to be a forward orientated battle.

New Zealand opted for a big, tough pack and two in form half backs in Fred Ah Kuoi and Shane Varley, who had a spell at Leigh later. As expected, the Kiwis came out with all guns blazing. Kevin Fisher was over the Lions try line after only three minutes. Three minutes after that Mark Graham blasted Gary Stephens out of his way and fed the supporting Fred Ah Kui who gave a wide pass to Olsen Filipaina and he, in turn, found Lewis Hudson steaming up at his shoulder and sent Dane O'Hara diving over for a brilliant try. The Lions hit back with a fine try from Steve Evans who accepted a long George Nicholls pass and beat three defenders with magnificent side steps to cross for a memorable try. Olsen Filipaina landed a long range penalty goal to give the Kiwis an 8–3 lead but in the final three minutes of the half the Lions sprang into scoring mode as Mike Smith scored by the corner flag and as the hooter sounded, David Ward released a fine one handed pass to Eric Hughes who chipped over James Leuluai's head, raced on and dribbled the ball to dive over in great style for George Fairbairn to tag on the extra two. This gave Great Britain an 11–8 lead at half time.

The second half proved to be a real forward battle with George Nicholls, Jeff Grayshon and Len Casey leading the way for the Lions while the Tamati cousins, Howie and Kevin, Mark Graham and Mark Broadhurst were outstanding for New Zealand. It was indeed Graham who scored one of his special tries, beating several defenders in a 30 yard run. Finishing the game the strongest and gradually taking a grip as the time ticked away, James Leuluai linked up from full back and raced over for a super try to which Olsen Filipaino added the conversion to give him three goals in the match. The Kiwis deserved their victory against a touring team already thinking of their homeward bound trip but there was one further game to be played against the strong and tough Auckland district side.

Elated by their success in the final Test, the Kiwi bosses selected a near Test strength side for the farewell game. The top Auckland players were included and the full Maori farewell traditions were catered for with Maori songs, before and after the game, Maori dancers in full war regalia and the singing of 'Now is the hour'. The friendliness stopped after the whistle to start the game but returned, warmly, on the ending of the game and the tour. Eric Ashton said a big thank you to his team of Lions who had not made it into the final Test team by selecting the following team for the final match of the tour, Keith Mumby; David Barends, John Woods, Peter Glynn, Roy Mathias; David Topliss, Alan Redfearn; John Burke, David Watkinson, Mel James, Brian Lockwood, Charlie Stone and Phil Hogan and the subs were Eric Hughes and Graham Liptrot. The tourists put on an organised, workmanlike performance to beat the Auckland side 18–10 and end the tour on a happy note. Almost all the players who had the good fortune to gain selection on any Lions tour will say that the education of any professional Rugby League player is incomplete without the experience of a tour. The memories, the comradeship, the lasting friendships made and the sheer enjoyment of this wonderful gift given by the touring team selectors is, in most cases, cherished for life.

This particular tour of 1979 was successful in as much as the Lions beat the majority of District and State sides who had the reputations and traditions of beating touring teams. The sting in the tail is that this side lost all three Tests against the Kangaroos. That alone is the reason for touring! Any player who toured and lost a Test series against the old enemy Australia will feel the same. But in almost all other reasons, being selected to tour is the zenith of a player's career, a wonderful achievement and a superb entry on anyone's CV.

7

YEARNING FOR WEMBLEY

We flew out of Auckland on 14 August and landed in Sydney to change aircraft and almost immediately flew out of Sydney heading for home. We arrived in Manchester on the 16 August and reported to Odsal on the 17 August for fitness checks ahead of the game at Fartown against Huddersfield in Sunday's Yorkshire Cup First round tie. Dave Barends, Alan Redfearn, Keith Mumby and I were declared fit but Len Casey had a knee problem after the final Test in Auckland and was declared unfit.

The tour had not been a financial success. Usually the pay out at the Tour's end was a share of the profits of the trip for each player and, whilst falling short of the word 'substantial', one expected a fair few quid from the RFL coffers. Jeff's share was the same as all the others, just a few pence above £43!

Jeff's wife Sue still has a laugh on recalling her surprise when Jeff opened his letter with the news of the share payout,

> Without expecting a fabulous amount, I had hoped for it to go some way in building a kitchen extension to our home. As it was it certainly turned out to be a bit disappointing, especially with Jeff being away for three months, but we managed and having him back safe and sound was a bonus.

Sunday 19th August saw Jeff pack down at loose forward behind Ian Van Bellen, Brian Noble, George Mordue, Alan Spencer and Neil Fox at Fartown in the straightforward 22–7 win to go into round two of the County Cup. Wakefield Trinity were the visitors to Odsal and what a shock result it was with Trinity completely overwhelming Bradford by the almost unbelievable score of 30–5.

Yorkshire County Versus Cumbria, Derwent Park, Workington, 29 September 1979

Jeff had been informed of his selection for Yorkshire County to play against Cumbria up in Derwent Park, Workington on Wednesday 29 September 1979 in the County Championship. This was Jeff's 10th appearance for the County and he was honoured by being asked to captain the Yorkshire side.

Jeff led from the front in an effort to win on his first outing as County captain but on the evening Cumbria were on top of their game. If there were any breaks to be given then referee Stan Wall offered more to the Cumbrians than to the Yorkies, not unfairly of course but because of the bounce of the ball. Yorkshire scored two fine tries through the pace of their talented backs, Andy Fletcher and Barry Banks, and three goals from the deadly marksman Mick Parrish. Tony Dean slotted over a neat drop goal to give the visitors their 13 points. The Cumbrian toughness and their determination on home soil allowed them to register three tries through Ian Ball, Eddie Bowman and Les Gorley and the four goals from Ian MacCorquodale totalled their 17. This gave them a hard earned victory on the night. The Yorkshire committee were full of praise for the effort put in by Jeff and his team and had some kind words to say especially to the credit of Jeff for his usual massive defensive display and the way in which he led the team throughout the game.

It was back to basics again up at Odsal as the new season resumed after the early County Championship matches. Outside the Yorkshire Cup Bradford still had plenty to play for as the John Player Trophy was about to start. But before that there were two league matches to negotiate. The newly promoted Hunslet welcomed Bradford Northern to Elland Road and gave Jeff and company a nasty shock by beating Northern 15–13. Revenge was gained against Wakefield Trinity a week after the defeat at Hunslet with a comprehensive 27–3 victory. Another week's progress saw the beginning of the John Player Trophy with Bradford playing Doncaster in round one over at Tatters Field. Northern negotiated this hurdle in fine style with a 48–0 win and progressed to another tough looking second round tie away to Keighley at Lawkholme Lane. But before that came arguably the toughest away fixture of the season, that of having to play at Knowsley Road, St Helens.

For this league game Bradford welcomed back their international forward Len Casey and with Len and Jeff the Northern forward defensive unit was strengthened immensely. Both teams seemed to be heading for further club honours and this league game was crucial to the league standing to maintain an early hold on a top position in the table. In a magnificent result for Bradford their try scorers were Keith Mumby, Len Casey and Eddie Oculicz, Steve Ferres kicked five goals and Ferres and Nigel Stephenson each dropped a goal. The sole scorer for Saints in this game was Harry Pinner who scored their try, kicked three goals and landed a drop goal in this super 21–10 win for Bradford.

Keighley proved tough opponents on their own ground in round two of the John Player. Jeff remembers:

The two early season defeats by Wakefield in the County Cup and Hunslet in the league game looked a bit silly after the trip to Saints and coming away with a great win. But it showed that playing with only a slight drop in concentration and determination any team can be vulnerable, home or away, against a team showing guts and character. Going to Lawkholme Lane was going to be hard and we had a word amongst ourselves, just to remind us of the basics required, before we set off for this cup tie in the John Player Trophy. The only changes from the team that beat Saints were Ian Van Bellen in at prop for Jimmy Thompson who was working, Dave Barends back on the wing for Denis Trotter with Denis and David Redfearn as subs.

The local 'derby' between us and Keighley always threw up some old scores to settle and this game was no exception. The tackles came in hard and fast with 'no prisoners' as the by-word. The game was played in true cup tie spirit on a pitch that was a shade on the muddy side so it was a slog for the pack. Keith Mumby, I remember, scored a very good solo try and it was nice for Peter Roe to register a try against his old club. Colin Forsyth bulldozed over for a try and Steve Ferres kicked three goals as we took a hold of the game in the second half and held on to win 15–9.

Again newspaper reports of this John Player tie from the *Telegraph & Argus* point out that the Bradford pack once again, with Colin Forsyth, Jeff and Len Casey, laid the foundation of the win by an outstanding performance. Jeff recalls:

> Being in the middle of a cup run, we had eyes on the draw for the next round whilst taking a peep at the fixtures in the league to give us an idea how hard the future looked. Home draws in cup ties help and we were in luck in the third round draw for the John Player by getting a home tie against the grand footballing side from Leigh.

The Leigh game was sandwiched between two tough games, Hull FC at the Boulevard and Warrington at Wilderspool. Neither venues were places to travel to with a faint heart! York were beaten at Odsal in the league 23–12 then came the tough game at The Boulevard.

Any trip to play at The Boulevard was a traumatic experience and what a hum-dinger of a game this was. Hull FC had invested heavily on top class players over the past two seasons. They had impressive players such as Charlie Stone, Steve Norton, 'Sammy' Lloyd, John Newlove, Clive Pickerill and Charlie Birdsall and as a result had gone through unbeaten the previous season in a strong second division. From the first whistle it was like a cup final replay! Not one player from either side was prepared to give an inch. Gaining ground by opposing forwards attempting breaks was met by unflinching defences and both sets of backs had no room whatsoever in which to work. It was a complete shutdown. Only twice in the whole 80 minutes was there the semblance of a scoring chance given, both falling to Bradford and both taken. First Alan Redfearn somehow managed to squeeze in by the corner flag then Jeff, using his formidable strength to smash a way through an almost impregnable array of tacklers, planted the ball down and enabled Bradford Northern to emerge as 6–4 winners of this titanic struggle.

The second incredibly tough league game was at Warrington two weeks later when another front line battle was fought out at Wilderspool when, yet again, both side's defences withstood terrific attacks to end up, this time, as a 10–8 defeat for Bradford. In between these two gigantic clashes was the quarter final of the John Player Trophy at Odsal against Leigh. Bradford strode through to the semi final with a fine 25–11 win to set up the semi final against Wakefield Trinity. The following match was the battle at Warrington. Then a week later Leigh came to Odsal for the second time in a fortnight to catch Northern on the hop and gain a tremendous, yet surprising, 17–15 win. Back to winning ways came Bradford the next week with a splendid 23–10 win over York at Clarence

Street, or Wiggington Road as it came to be known.

The game on 17th November was one of the most important games for quite some time for Bradford Northern. This was the semi final of the John Player Trophy. The Bradford side was specially selected to do a job on Wakefield Trinity and the result was a comfortable 16–3 win for Bradford, with Alan Redfearn (2) and Derrick Parker scoring tries and Steve Ferres kicking three goals and a drop goal.

Jeff well remembers this period of activity within the Odsal club:

> Division one of the Rugby Football League was very competitive with all the big clubs chasing every trophy and the slightly lesser clubs all up for it when the cup ties came around. This highly competitive spirit, many a time, spilled over into the league fixtures and made for some close games. After our win over Trinity in the John Player semi I remember playing four or five very hard and tough matches on the trot.

They were tough indeed, Castleford away, Saints at Home, Wigan away, Hull Kingston Rovers at home and Leeds at Odsal constituted the next five league games for Bradford.

This tough run began with defeat at Castleford by 11–6. Jeff recalls the details:

> This was one we could have won, we made several try scoring chances but wasted them. We were too eager and instead of playing steadily, we rushed at the chances and missed them. But against Saints two days later we controlled our game better and in fact I remember we controlled Saints which is more to the point. It was a close run thing again with us winning 13–9. The next game was against one of the clubs on its own ground that I loved to play against, Wigan at Central Park. There always seemed to be plenty of room on that big pitch and although it meant lots of hard work on defence as the Wigan teams always moved the ball well, it was

always a ground which was a favourite of mine. As it was I had a knock on my shoulder in the Saints game and although it responded to treatment, Peter thought it better to give it a rest with the John Player final and a couple of stiff league games coming up soon.

Despite losing Jeff for this game, Bradford came out of this Wigan fixture with a fine 13–2 win. He returned the following week for the home game against Hull Kingston Rovers only to be on the losing side in one of the rare home defeats. Jeff indeed proved his return to fitness with a strong game in which he registered the Bradford try in the 14–5 loss, admitting:

> I was upset with the defeat by Hull Kingston Rovers even though I knew I had played well enough after the shoulder injury. Now we had to beat Leeds at Odsal to keep up in the top three and maintain our chances of finishing top of the league come the end of the season.

This key match against the Loiners turned out to be another savage encounter. Both teams tackled their hearts out in a very evenly contested game and each side managed only one try apiece, Phil Cookson for Leeds and Nigel Stephenson for Bradford. The difference was in the goal kicking as Willie Oulton managed one for Leeds against the two from Keith Mumby for Northern. Jeff recalls, 'This was a good win for us. The score of 7–5 showed just how tight a game it was but we held out against a strong finish by Leeds to claim the points'. The next game too was a nail biter when Bradford travelled to Salford and in a thrilling game the men from Odsal again demonstrated a strong desire to win by hanging onto a three point advantage and held on for a 14–11 win. Three days later Bradford had a slightly easier passage against Blackpool

Borough who had gained promotion from division two the previous season. They won the game at Odsal 28–nil.

Bradford Northern Versus Widnes, John Player Trophy Final, Headingley, Leeds, 5 January 1980

The final of the John Player Trophy was played at Headingley on 5 January 1980 between Bradford Northern and Widnes. The 'Chemics' were making their fifth appearance in this final and it was the ninth final of this popular competition, thus showing the strength of the Widnes side and their determination to command this trophy yet again for a third win. 'Bradford had won this trophy back in 1974–75 and beat Widnes in that final,' recalled Jeff. 'It was a close call that day with Northern winning 3–2 and we hoped that it would not be as close in this one.' Comparing the combined strength of both teams, this final had all the hallmarks of a close run battle. Of the 30 players on view, 17 were international footballers. At the end of this season Bradford Northern had topped the League Leaders' table with Widnes in second place, demonstrating how close to each other these teams were.

But on this cold, damp January afternoon, the season was only half way through and there were cups and trophies to be played for. Try scoring chances were at a premium with the defences working overtime. Derek Parker did score the only try of the game with a typically strong surge to the line and with Keith Mumby adding a goal and Nigel Stephenson dropping a neat goal, Bradford Northern lifted the trophy with a score of 6–nil. With the Bradford pack gradually getting on top and just staying the course that bit longer than Widnes, the result was considered fair. Len Casey took the Man of the Match award for his enthusiastic performance. Sadly this was the final Bradford Northern game for that great forward Len

Casey who was transferred to Hull Kingston Rovers shortly after. Jeff remembers the time well:

> After the success against Widnes in the John Player we embarked on a six match winning run against some very good sides in real close games. I was sorry to see Len Casey move on as he was, and still is, a good mate. This kind of tough opposition helped in keeping us focused as the Challenge Cup was coming up in the near future and there were several of us who wanted to add the experience of a Wembley final to our CV. We gained revenge on Hull Kingston Rovers with a cracking 10–9 victory across at Craven Park and after they had walloped us at Odsal in the league this result tasted all the sweeter. The Challenge Cup arrived on 10 February with a trip to the seaside to take on Blackpool Borough at Borough Park. We negotiated this awkward hurdle with a 26–7 win and continued our good run with a super win against Hull FC at Odsal by 12–5. The following week we had to travel to Hilton Park, not the easiest of games by a long chalk, to play Leigh.
>
> This was another tough outing where we had to defend for long spells before winning narrowly 11–8. These close games had sharpened up the team and we needed to be razor sharp when we heard the draw for round two of the Challenge Cup. We had drawn arguably the hardest tie, St Helens away! The newspapers were calling it the match of the decade and were insisting that the winners of the cup would come from this game. I suppose that if you want to win the Challenge Cup then you have to beat teams like St Helens, so hoping that all these tough games had worked for us, we set our stall out to go in the correct frame of mind. On 23rd February we lined up at Knowsley Road determined to stick to our guns.

To say this was a great cup tie would do the match a disservice. It was a terrific cup tie with all the trimmings. A few missed scoring chances, and there were some try saving tackles, brilliant attacking plays, great foraging work by both packs and sweeping backs moves that had the 9,000 spectators cheering their heads off. Les Gant was a Bradford hero scoring two cracking tries and Colin Forsyth, who scored many tries in his career, can't have scored a better one than when he crashed over for Nigel Stephenson to kick his only goal of the game. This gave Bradford their 11 points. Saints had two tries scored by the excellent Peter Glynn and two Harry Pinner goals giving them their 10 points. That is how close it was in this great 11–10 win for Bradford. Still, even after this wonderful win, Jeff would not allow himself to think of a Wembley visit. The following Wednesday evening Bradford entertained Castleford at Odsal in the league match and battled through to beat Cas 12–3, albeit without Jeff as he had gained selection for England to play in the 1980 European Championship. On top of this the news came through that Bradford had drawn Hull FC at Odsal in round three of the Challenge Cup. This was wonderful news, a home draw in the third and most crucial of cup rounds! It was a good time for Jeff on a personal level as he made a comeback into international Rugby League.

England Versus Wales, European Championship, Craven Park, Hull, 29 February 1980

The next international game was England versus Wales at Craven Park. Jeff was selected as substitute forward. This European Championship involved three countries, England, Wales and France. Wales had lost to France 21–7 at Naughton Park, Widnes. Now England were looking to beat both Wales and France to win the Championship outright. Wales proved to be no match on the day for a confident and faster England who won this game by a convincing 26–9. The tries for England were scored by George Fairbairn, John Joyner and Roy Holdstock. Keith Rayne and Fairbairn kicked six goals and

Harry Pinner two drop goals. Wales replied with a try by Brian Juliff and three goals from Paul Woods. Jeff played for the final 13 minutes and tackled with his usual effectiveness, supporting and running well.

It was back to bread and butter league football after the international but Jeff missed the home win against Castleford because of slight pull to his 'bad' leg which he injured in Australia when at Cronulla. A defeat at the hands of Wakefield Trinity at Belle Vue 18–15 was explained away in that the team had their minds on the next game—the vital third round Challenge Cup tie at Odsal against Hull FC. There was an almost full house at the Bradford ground to witness a real old fashioned cup tie. The experienced Hull FC coach, Arthur Bunting, had built up a strong pack of forwards and had a clever stand off half in John Newlove.

The strength of the Hull FC side though was in their tough forwards with the likes of Keith Tindall, Ron Wileman, Vince Farrar, Charlie Stone, 'Sammy' Lloyd, Steve Norton and Charlie Birdsall and waiting in the wings an excellent junior called Lee Crooks. Bradford had done everything right in this cup run. They even had the luck of the draw being at home in the hardest of all the cup rounds, the third. Peter went for his tried and tested team with his key players in place and prepared his team perfectly for this absolutely crucial crunch game. Unfortunately sometimes in life, no matter how well you prepare and no matter how good a player you may be, fate seems to deny you the things you yearn for most of all in your career. No matter how hard you try, the object of your achievements is always just out of reach. This seems to be the case for Jeff in his search for the 'Holy Grail' of every professional Rugby League player, that of representing his club in the Challenge Cup final at Wembley. Players with hardly half the ability of Jeff have trod that hallowed turf more than once in their careers. But despite several semi final appearances and playing for teams who looked odds on certainties to progress all the way, fate had the final say and the excellent international forward Jeff Grayshon never achieved his goal of a Wembley appearance.

The third round cup tie against Hull FC was a case in point as all the cards were dealt to Bradford but in the closest of games Hull FC went through to the semi final on the back of a 3–nil win in this brutal game. Hull FC went on to play Widnes in the semi final and won 10–5. The other semi finalists that season were Hull Kingston Rovers against the club I was coaching at the time, Halifax. Hull KR went through to play Hull FC at Wembley. This led to the famous sign planted on the entrance of the motorway at Hull leading to the London bound M1, 'Will the last one out turn off the lights?'

The defeat by Hull FC in that third round tie was a devastating blow to Jeff:

> I really thought that with us being at home we could rise to the occasion and overcome the Hull lads. We knew it would be a hard task as they had a very good side but so did we and with the score so close it was obvious that we could have won if we had taken the few chances that came our way. But another chance had come and gone and although I didn't really believe in fate, after this game I began to wonder! I had listened to players tell of the Wembley experience for years. Although I had made the grade in international football and been to Australia and New Zealand on tour, played in Australia at club level and represented my county, the adventure and wonderful experience of playing at Wembley and all the trimmings that go with a Challenge Cup final seemed out of reach. This was something I had to put behind me and I had to concentrate on the future not the past!

England Versus France, European Championship, Narbonne, 16 March 1980

Jeff missed the following game for Northern up at Workington Town as he was involved in the England versus France deciding game in the European Championship in Narbonne.

If anyone thought this game would be a 'walk over' for England then they were sadly mistaken. The French fought like tigers to lift this championship trophy and their forwards, led by the excellent Joel Roosebrouck, really took the game to the English pack. So tight was the tackling that the only chance that came England's way in the first half was a well taken effort by Steve Evans. He crossed for a try about half way through the first half after Jeff and Peter Smith had combined to send Mike Smith clean away and Hull Kingston Rovers excellent middle back sent Steve Evans racing over for an unconverted try. A penalty goal by Tranier took the score to 3–2 in England's favour and a snap drop goal by the industrious Alan Redfearn saw England home to a very close 4–2 victory. Jeff said:

> I had played against France on several occasions and without doubt this was the toughest game by far. Their tackling was fierce and there were always two or three defenders in on every tackle. David Ward led the way for us with a real captain's knock and to be honest there was not one weak link in our defence. It's a good job as the French let us have it when they carried the ball too. One or two of Billy Thompson's decisions angered the French but mostly it was the old problem of slight differences in the interpretation of the laws of the game between the two countries. As it was this victory gave us the European Championship title and that was sweet!

Three days later, on the Wednesday evening, Bradford Northern faced the daunting trip away to play Widnes at

Naughton Park and both Alan Redfearn and Jeff were back in harness for the club. If the reader seems to think that the close scores in these games are fictitious, I can assure you that in those days the scores in the games between the top clubs usually were close. The result at Widnes was a great 11–10 victory for Bradford in a nail biting match. Derek Parker and David Readfearn scored tries and Nigel Stephenson kicked two goals and dropped one.

After the victory at Widnes, three superb wins in the league for Bradford Northern followed, Salford at Odsal by 15–nil, Wigan at Odsal 16–5 and a magnificent 7–2 win at Headingley against the old enemy Leeds. Bradford were now pushing strongly to finish top of the league at the season's end and were hoping to secure the League Leaders trophy. To finish in that lofty position, Bradford had to gain top results in these kinds of games and for once Bradford had a stroke of luck in that Leeds were very much under strength because of injuries. Despite Leeds not being at full strength in their pack it was a sterling performance by Bradford with David Barends scoring their try and Nigel Stephenson kicking two goals.

Blackpool Borough at the seaside made Bradford work hard for Northern's 15–14 win. Three days later Warrington surprised Bradford with a gutsy performance at Wilderspool beating Northern 10–4. It was now a two horse race for the League Leaders trophy between Bradford and Widnes. They were clear from Hull FC and Salford in third and fourth place, but Bradford had their final three league games of the season at Odsal. The first of these games was against Workington Town who were beaten 32–15. The second game was against Hunslet who had beaten Bradford at Elland Road 15–13. But Bradford, with the bit between their teeth, were in a different frame of mind for this game and ran out easy 41–16 winners. By beating Hunslet it meant that Bradford had secured first place on the league ladder. This result pleased Peter Fox as the team finishing first was the most consistent team of the season.

Although the disappointment in the Challenge Cup still rankled, the League Leaders trophy was still a fine achievement and with the play offs still to come the league championship was still an option. The final league game of the season, would you believe, was against Widnes at Odsal. Imagine the impact of this game if it had been for the League Leaders title! As it was Bradford Northern had already won this race allowing Peter Fox to rest most of his key players for the play offs which were in six days time. So a most unusual Bradford team took the field that afternoon, Ferres; McLean, Oculicz, Gant, Alan Parker; Carroll, Robinson; Ian Van Bellen, Noble, Thompson, Gary Van Bellen, Spencer and Hale. Subs: Forsyth and Jeff Grayshon. The result was a 21–5 win for Widnes. An unusual feature of Bradford's five points was a rare drop goal by Jimmy Thompson!

So the time had arrived for the play offs. Bradford were at home to St Helens in the 1st v 8th clubs first round. Now back to their normal team, Bradford beat the Saints 30–nil. The semi finals of this competition were played on a two legged system with Bradford playing Leigh home and away in one semi final and in the other Widnes played Leeds'. Bradford won at Hilton Park, Leigh 14–12, and at Odsal in the second leg they won again 17–4 giving an aggregate score of Bradford 31 Leigh 16. In the other semi final Widnes lost 14–4 at Headingley but won an exciting second leg at Naughton Park 14–3 going through to the final on a 18–17 aggregate.

Bradford Versus Widnes, Premiership Trophy Final, Station Road, Swinton, 17 May 1980

The final between Bradford and Widnes turned out to be a disaster for Bradford. Widnes played brilliantly to lift the trophy with tries by Elwell, Bentley, Write, Aspey and Gorley with a goal from Mick Burke and drop goals from Elwell and Eckersley. In reply Northern posted a try from Dave Redfearn converted by Keith Mumby. The 19–5 result showed the Chemics' class on the day but it didn't do justice to Bradford's season which had been one of highs and lows for Jeff and his team mates. That elusive Wembley appearance had once again evaded Jeff's grasp but as the big forward would say, 'There's always next season!'

* * * * *

The 1980–81 season began with a 10–6 win for Bradford against Batley in the Yorkshire Cup at Odsal. Round two of the County Cup was against Huddersfield at Fartown, a game I remember vividly. I had joined Huddersfield as coach in the close season and knew that it would take a massive effort on my team's behalf to hold this powerful Bradford side, especially as Huddersfield were looked on as a mid table second division side. But hold them we did and, thanks to two superb Peter Cramp tries and with a whole hearted defence working overtime, Huddersfield gained a memorable 20–13 victory. A defeat at St Helens 16–6 followed the shock result at Fartown but after that, apart from losing the odd tough game, Bradford marched on to perform heroically in the last quarter of the league programme to capture, for the second year running, the League Leaders trophy for finishing top of the league. Oldham were beaten at Odsal 21–10 and a great 12–10 win up in Barrow at Craven Park was earned in another close game. The 1980 New Zealand tourists arrived and looked a decent side in their early games. Bradford had three games to play in the league before the Kiwis visited Odsal to play Northern.

Yorkshire Versus Cumbria, County Championship, Craven Park, Hull, 17 September 1980

After the Barrow away game, Jeff was called into the Yorkshire County side to play Cumbria in the County Championship at Hull Kingston Rovers' ground, Craven Park. Jeff was thrilled to be named captain of Yorkshire, as one of his early ambitions was to play for the County and now, as captain, his wish had been more than granted. It was on Wednesday 17th September that Jeff proudly led out his Yorkshire team, coached by Arthur Keegan formally of Hull FC, Bramley and Batley. The Cumbrian coach was that grand former international and both Whitehaven and Workington half back, Phil Kitchen.

Yorkshire went into an early lead when Andy Fletcher sprinted over after swift Yorkshire handling gave him space down the touchline, Steve Quinn landed a great conversion from wide out. But the home side were drawn into making this a forward battle and this was the Cumbrian strength. With the two big props Bowman and Cunningham running amok and the Gorley brothers following suit Cumbria began to get on top and dictate the game. Peter Gorley forced his way over then Alan McCurrie dummied his way through two defenders to score and with Ian Ball kicking both goals then dropping a neat goal Yorkshire were up against it. Kevin Dick replied with a strong try from dummy half and Quinn converted. Arnie Walker, renowned for his strong running near the try line did just that and crashed over for a clever try, Ball converting giving Cumbria 16 points. Kevin Dick landed two towering drop goals and Quinn landed two penalty goals to give the game a rousing finish at 16 points all. Suddenly prop forward John Cunningham hit a tremendous drop goal that soared high above the cross bar to give Cumbria the slender advantage they had deserved. When the whistle blew to end the game the Cumbrian players danced with joy as this result had meant so much to the game up in the North West. Yorkshire were beaten 17–16.

Jeff's statistics as a player proved his determination, devotion and loyalty to the game whichever team he was serving. In this season of 1980–81 Jeff played in 31 of Bradford Northern's 36 league and cup games as well as representing Yorkshire and Great Britain. His durability as a hard working forward and his ability to quickly overcome the bumps and bruises received in the games he played in are testimony to both his attitude and natural toughness.

Lancashire Versus Yorkshire, County Championship, Naughton Park, Widnes, 24 September 1980

The County Championship resumed on 24th September 1980 with the traditionally tough game against Lancashire at Naughton Park, Widnes. Lancashire's selectors were looking to introduce some young blood into inter County Rugby League and gave several up and coming youngsters their chance. Again Jeff skippered the Yorkshire side and spun the coin with Lancashire captain Mick Adams. He recalls:

> I really wanted to win this one with the fierce rivalry between the Counties plus a bumper sponsorship from the Hoover Company of £1,000 to the Championship winners. But on the night Lancashire deserved their 17–9 win.

Lancashire's try scorers were Terry Bilsbury, Neil Holding and Jimmy Hornby with four goals from Colin Whitfield. The

Yorkshire reply came from an Andy Fletcher try and three goals from Steve Quinn.

Jeff was back at work the following week at the brickworks only to be on duty again four days after the County game as Bradford took on Leigh at Odsal. Jeff was a try scorer both in the 22–2 win for Northern and again the next week in the tough drawn game, 15 points apiece, at Belle Vue, Wakefield. Three hard games faced Bradford now, Leeds at home, Hull Kingston Rovers away and the New Zealand touring team.

Leeds were beaten 11–5 in another difficult match (nothing new when these two traditionally great sides met). The Leeds side were in a transitional period and about to venture into the transfer market. Although a few of their players were approaching the end of their careers, Leeds were still a dangerous outfit with quite a bit of pace in the backs and two good half backs. The problems for Leeds were in the pack. The forwards at Headingley were a touch on the light side apart from the big, strong Mick Harrison. Facing this Leeds side was a Bradford team which had lost two and drawn one in seven games. Bradford gradually out muscled Leeds and a try by Gary Hale and four Jimmy Fiddler goals gave the home side 11 points. This was against a Kevin Dick try and one goal from Willie Oulton giving Leeds 5 points. Peter Fox went with the same team to play Hull Kingston Rovers at Craven Park a week later changing only his subs bringing in Steve Ferres and Denis Trotter for Phil Sanderson and Ian Van Bellen. The result was a sudden shock as Hull Kingston Rovers' big pack did to Bradford what Bradford had done to Leeds and The Robins ran out winners 28–14.

The final game of the tough trilogy was against the Kiwi tourists. In an effort to keep his key players fresh, and save the legs of his pack for the tough future league games, Peter Fox switched his team around for this game. He rested his two experienced forwards, Jimmy Thompson and Jeff Grayshon along with full back Keith Mumby. Young Green came in for Mumby, Les Gant moved to centre to partner the strong Derek Parker with David Barrends and Alan Parker on the wings, Alan coming under the care of brother Derek. Jimmy Fiddler moved across to field side prop and Phil Sanderson took the number 10 jersey. The quick Denis Trotter took Jeff's place and the subs were Steve Ferres and Gary Hale. This patched up Northern team covered themselves with glory as they took on the Kiwis and were victorious with a magnificent 15–10 win.

In the league games Bradford struggled to achieve consistency. In the previous two seasons with top of the league as their ambition the team had embarked on runs of wins against all the top clubs, both home and away. This season was different. Jeff recalls:

> We could still manage the odd very good win but putting this type of win back to back and going on to climb to the top of the league was seemingly beyond us. We all wondered why. Could it be that our key forwards were all ageing together? Our strongest pack were all turned 30 plus, Jimmy Thompson, Ian Van Bellen, myself and Keith Bridges. There were still some good young forwards coming through, Gary Van Bellen, Phil Jackson, Denis Trotter and one or two in the 'A' team but we needed an injection as soon as possible to halt the decline.

Warrington were beaten at Wilderspool 10–7 and Barrow at Odsal a week later by 13–5. But the inconsistency returned with consecutive defeats by Oldham at the Watersheddings 9–2, Hull FC at The Boulevard in the first round of the John Player Trophy 12–0, Hull Kingston Rovers at Odsal 26–7 and Salford at The Willows 18–9. The point made earlier about Jeff's dedication to his club was shown when for the Great

Britain v New Zealand game in the first Test played at Wigan, Jeff was selected to play in the second row. The day after a fearsomely hard game, Jeff played for Bradford Northern in the league game in the win over Salford at Odsal.

Great Britain Versus New Zealand, First Test, Central Park, Wigan, 18 October 1980

The Test at Wigan illustrated that the improvement threatened by the Kiwis had arrived. With still more top class youngsters coming through at home the men in Black and White were travelling quickly enough in international Rugby League to soon be pushing the mighty Australia all the way in their annual Trans Tasman Test series. Jeff recollected that:

> All the talk in club football was about how good some of these Kiwis were. The results coming out of New Zealand seemed to prove that the New Zealand game had taken an upsurge and almost unbelievably was challenging Rugby Union for TV time in Test matches.

The Great Britain side had another new captain in George Fairbairn and gave caps to seven new internationals. The new caps, Chris Camilleri, Keith Bentley, Steve Hartley, Kevin Dick, Roy Holdstock, Les Gorley and Harry Pinner had all earned their spurs over some years with good clubs and all had winning experience in club football.

Almost typical of those tough Test matches, the first scrum ignited like a time bomb and a fierce brawl ensued. Fights erupted amongst the two packs of forwards who seemed to enjoy knocking the corners off each other. Sanity resumed and the Kiwis showed some fine forward play. Kevin Tamati and Mark Graham were particularly effective working together and creating openings in the home defence. George Fairbairn's two penalty goals gave Great Britain a slender lead but Fred Ah Koi scrambled over for a try and Gordon Smith's conversion gave the Kiwis a one point advantage. Soon after Mark Graham broke clear and fed the supporting Tony Coll who raced to the posts, Smith converting. The half time score was 10–9 to New Zealand as John Joyner and Kevin Dick combined to send over Chris Camilleri whose try was improved by Fairbairn as the hooter sounded.

Gordon Smith added a penalty goal as things warmed up again with Trevor Skerrett and Kevin Tamati battling it out. Against the run of play, the Brits managed to take the lead with a try from Mike Smith after Len Casey, Jeff and Harry Pinner opened the Kiwi defence, Fairbairn converting. Now ahead 14–12, it appeared that the home side may well steal a victory but with just four minutes remaining Gordon Smith levelled the score with a long range penalty goal. Paul Rylance, the respected writer for the *Daily Telegraph* said the Kiwis were overall the better side as their speed, awareness and fearless running caused the Lions great problems. Rugby League historian, Robert Gate is of a similar opinion in his description of this game in *Rugby League Lions, 100 years of Test Matches*. However the result meant that the series was still wide open.

Great Britain Versus New Zealand, Second Test, Odsal Stadium, Bradford, 2 November 1980

The second Test against the Kiwis was played on 2nd November at Odsal Stadium. This was the last time a Test match was played at the old ground and it happened to be one of the Lions' worst performances for many years. New Zealand won this Test with a gutsy exhibition of tough tackling and honest hard running and to quote Robert Gate, 'Great Britain's performance was truly awful'. Another experienced writer,

Trevor Watson of the *Yorkshire Evening Post*, hit the nail on the head as he had to report that 'Britain are in danger of becoming a second class Rugby League nation'. George Faibairn kicked four goals to give the Lions their 8 points but the Kiwi scorers were Mike O'Donnell and Dane O'Hara with a try apiece and Gordon Smith kicked three goals. This gave New Zealand a 12–8 win and wholesale changes were made to the Great Britain side for the final Test at Headingley.

Great Britain Versus New Zealand, Third Test, Headingley, Leeds, 15 November 1980

Jeff was a casualty for this game along with George Fairbairn, Mike Smith, Chris Camilleri, Ken Kelly, Kevin Dick, Roy Holdstock, Glyn Shaw and Harry Pinner. Ken Kelly [Warrington] and Roy Holdstock [Hull Kingston Rovers] acted as subs. Mick Burke [Widnes] came in at full back, John Atkinson [Leeds] resumed on the wing with Steve Evans [Featherstone Rovers] as his centre. John Woods [Leigh] and Arnie Walker [Whitehaven] were the two half backs, Trevor Skerrett [Hull FC] and Len Casey [Hull Kingston Rovers] were the props with Mick Adams [Widnes] and Peter Gorley [St Helens] in the second row and Steve Norton [Hull FC] back in at loose forward. Des Drummond crossed twice for tries and Mick Burke kicked two goals in the 10–2 win for the Lions, Gordon Smith managed one goal for the Kiwis.

* * * * *

Bradford were back on song against St Helens at Odsal winning 11–nil, then scored a 'double' over Halifax, 10–5 on Boxing Day at Thrum Hall and two days later 19–10 at Odsal. Two away defeats against Castleford 19–18 and Widnes 10–2 slowed them a wee bit but a good win against Workington Town 15–10 and a great 7–6 win at Odsal against Wakefield Trinity put Northern back in the top six. Featherstone Rovers were beaten 21–19 at Odsal, Jeff being a try scorer and the usual hard fight at The Boulevard saw Hull FC the victors by 10–9. Another trauma in the Challenge Cup occurred when Salford beat Bradford at The Willows 17–13 in the first round bringing another blow to Jeff's long ambition. Leigh played well to beat Bradford at Hilton Park 18–14 but Northern finished the season with a flourish to win the next seven league games ending, once again, in top league spot to maintain their League Leaders trophy. The wins came thick and fast. Winning games included Castleford at home (13–3), Workington Town away (14–13), Warrington at Odsal (26–7), Featherstone Rovers at Post Office Road (22–18) with Jeff scoring two tries. There was a real tough game following Featherstone, Widnes at Odsal (won 13–5), then came a great win over the old enemy, Leeds at Headingley (26–18) and lastly a final win in the league against Hull FC (35–18).

The Championship play off had St Helens coming to Odsal in round one. Having been knocked out of all the season's previous cup competitions early, Bradford Northern wanted to win the Championship for their supporters and to cement the hard work by winning the League Leaders trophy. On a bright afternoon Bradford lined up: Keith Mumby; David Barends, David Readfearn, Derek Parker, Alan Parker; Nigel Stephenson, Alan Redfearn; Jimmy Thompson, 'Tiger' Handforth, Phil Sanderson, Jeff Grayshon, Phil Jackson and Graham Idle, the subs were, Gary Hale and Jim Fiddler. St Helens had done well to finish in the top eight as they were in the process of redevelopment and their side was a comparatively young one. But despite the advantage of 'experience', the game was another disappointment for Jeff and his team mates for, try as they might, the young Saints would not surrender and two tries by Steve Peters with Harry Pinner kicking two goals and dropping two goal saw them gain a great 14–12 win. Phil Jackson and Phil Sanderson crossed for Northern and Keith Mumby kicked three goals.

So another season ended and a suggestion from Peter Fox had Jeff thinking. He was much bigger now than when he started with Dewsbury but he'd lost a touch of pace after his knee reconstruction in Australia. This coupled with his extensive experience in top level international and County games led Peter to ask Jeff to consider a positional change. The coach suggested a move to open side prop might add years onto Jeff's playing career. As there was a shortage of good number 8s around, any sort of decent form could open the door for further international places.

In the close season Bradford had lost the services of Jimmy Thompson, Nigel Stephenson and Steve Ferres but Peter Fox was covered in the front row by Jeff, who decided to try the change of position, and Ian Van Bellen who was still playing well. At hooker was the up and coming Brian Noble along with 'Tiger' Handforth and Keith Bridges although Keith had struggled with various injuries throughout the season. Jeff recalls:

> I thought over Peter's suggestion and I decided that he'd never put me wrong before and it seemed a sensible idea, so I got down to learning the art of the field side prop. I had never realised, in all the years I had played, the extent of the skills needed by a field side prop. Strength was the obvious requirement but there were other skills like footwork and angling of the body pushing inwards and upwards into the opposition hooker or field side prop to give the hooker room in which to win the ball. The field

side prop also needed the ability to hold the opposite prop or hooker up, push opponents backwards with a hooker swung around their neck, take all the weight of the other pack and at the same time hook the ball out with another foot should it be in front of you! There was nothing to it!

I practised hard all through the pre season but it was learning at the coal face that mattered, gaining that vital experience in the, then, crucial position of open, or field side prop. The young spectator today can't realise the importance of a good open side prop as today's scrummages are non competitive so the props just have to stand there. A good scrummaging open side prop was worth his weight in gold to his team as it was he, nine times out of 10, who won the ball in those tough, fierce and sometimes brutal clashes. Hookers will deny this but they know it is perfectly true.

So Jeff and his team mates began the 1981–82 season in good spirits and Jeff was looking forward to beginning a new section of his career in the totally new environment of a front rower. He was no longer a tall, slim, quick running almost centre like back rower. Jeff was now a big, strong man who was well respected by opponents facing him. Any fears Jeff had about this new position were dispelled after a few minutes playing in the first round of the Yorkshire Cup at Thrum Hall, Halifax. Playing much nearer each play the ball gave Jeff more of the ball and allowed him to quickly develop his close in ball handling techniques. He also began to work well with the dummy half, either Brian Noble or Alan Redfearn, to great effect. Being near the ball in close in play meant Jeff also sharpened his short passing game and his physical presence, strength and great pair of hands allowed him to develop what became his trade mark play for the remainder of his career, that of being an expert ball distributor to his supporting forwards.

His debut as a prop in the game at Halifax saw Jeff score a

try and make a couple for the young, fast moving player who was also making his first team debut, Dick Jasiewicz. Another player who made a try scoring debut that day was a young centre called Ellery Hanley.

A week later Bradford travelled across to play Leeds at Headingley in the second round of the County Cup. In this game Jeff scored Bradford's only try in a great 11–5 win. In this tough 'derby' cup tie, Keith Mumby kicked four goals to go with Jeff's try to make up Bradford's 11 points and Kevin Dick scored all the Leeds points with a try and a goal.

The league season started the following week with the no nonsense Widnes team visiting Odsal bringing Jeff into direct opposition with the hard man, Brian Hogan. Honours were even in this department but Widnes won a tight game 12–11. Bradford then travelled to Craven Park to take on Hull Kingston Rovers in the semi final of the Yorkshire Cup and Jeff scored a vital try in the super 12–11 win for Bradford.

Yorkshire Versus Lancashire, County Championship, Wheldon Road, Castleford, 9 September 1981

Jeff's move to open side prop had been monitored by the County selectors and his good form had convinced them that with his experience at this level he would be the man to play against Lancashire at Castleford in the County Championship. Yorkshire had some quick three quarters, two experienced half backs and a big speedy pack of forwards. Hoover had increased their sponsorship to £1,250 and Yorkshire were on £75 per man to win the game and win it they did with a score of 21–15. Try scorers for Yorkshire were Keith Mumby, John Joyner (2), Les Dyl and David Ward. Lancashire scorers were David Finch (kicking three goals), Des Drummond (two tries),

Keith Bentley (try) and Colin Whitfield (three goals). Jeff recalls this game:

> It was my first representative game as a prop forward and I was up against Mike O'Neill of Widnes, then a young, strong forward. I played near to the play the ball and cleared my own line as one did in those days and with the likes of Steve Norton, David Finch, big John Millington and Peter Smith I was never without support when offering the short pass whilst stood in the tackle. David Ward's passes from dummy half were as good as ever and I was surprised at the number of times Steve Nash raced up in support on the fringes of the Lancashire forward defensive screen. We knew the danger of the young Andy Gregory and the power and high work rate of Mick Adams, Brian Case and Ian Potter and also the skills of Harry Pinner at loose forward and we managed to cover the Lancashire strengths and exploit a few of their weaknesses. I remember our backs playing particularly well with John Joyner and Les Dyl being in great form in the centres.

The win over Hull KR in the Yorkshire Cup semi final took Bradford into the final to play Castleford at Headingley on 3 October 1981. Before that some important league games had to be negotiated. Leigh beat Bradford at Hilton Park 17–14 and Hull Kingston Rovers gained revenge for the defeat in the County Cup by playing excellent football at Odsal to win 19–8. Back on the winning track a week after the Hull Kingston Rovers defeat, Bradford won a real tough battle with a score of 8–7 up at Whitehaven with battles and stand up fights amongst the teams. Jeff and Ellery Hanley were the try scorers in the home win against Wigan with Ellery also kicking three goals in the 12–5 victory.

Bradford Versus Castleford, Yorkshire Cup Final, Headingley, Leeds, 3 October 1981

Then came the Yorkshire Cup final game against Castleford. Jeff remembers:

> Castleford were one of those teams that were hard to beat. They never gave up in both attack and defence. The area around the town produced top youngsters who normally found it easy to settle into first team rugby after making debut. They were always a keen side and the younger players all knew the game inside out. Rugby League is in the blood of any kid from Castleford and is a great area for the game to thrive. This was a typical hard working Castleford side. Barry Johnson took their pack running forward all the game. Kevin Ward was a handful and David Finch was as quick as ever running wide out. Andy Timson and Bob Spurr were as busy as ever doing their tackling and running hard at us. On the day Castleford deserved their 10–5 win but as the score suggests, if we had taken our chances we could have lifted the County Cup but, fair play to Castleford, they won the cup on merit.

The defeat to Castleford had a negative effect on Northern's performance over the next few weeks. Maybe confidence was knocked but having got so close to picking up silverware early in the season, Bradford then seemed to go through a period of inconsistency as Jeff explains:

> The following week we came a cropper at St Helens in the league game as they rammed into us and caught us still rubbing our wounds from the Cup final. Saints won this game 20–8. Rochdale Hornets were our opponents in the first round of the John Player Trophy at the Athletic Grounds and we progressed 19–3. We won another tough league game against Barrow at Odsal 22–10 but the following week we travelled up to Craven Park, Barrow to play the 'Shipbuilders' again, this time in the John Player. This game was totally different to the week before. In the league meeting at Odsal we were given room in which to play our normal game. We had no room at all in this cup tie as the Barrow tacklers were all

over us like a rash and although the score looked close, we were never in the hunt.

We made the long trek home, kicking ourselves for being so complacent and not approaching this game with our usual professional attitude. We had been a bit too sloppy and had not imposed ourselves upon Barrow as we were asked to do by Peter. Possibly it was the aftermath of our Yorkshire Cup defeat by Castleford but we had to snap out of it quickly as any form of weakness, either mental or physical would be targeted in this tough first division of league matches. Barrow had won the John Player tie 8–0. The Barrow defeat was the start of a 15 day nightmare for us at Odsal as there followed two defeats in the league, at Belle Vue, Wakefield Trinity 11–8 and at home to St Helens by 20–8.

There is no stranger game in the world than Rugby League Football and whilst Jeff and company were wondering where the next win would come from they had one of the toughest trips in league football to The Boulevard to take on Hull FC. Lo and behold, the Bradford lads played their hearts out and came away with a fine 13–10 victory. Jeff set the team on the right path as he served up one of his special tries which had the 'Threp'ney Stand' cheering.

Whitehaven were beaten at Odsal 18–5 and it was international call up time again for Jeff. One of the directors at Odsal had marked Jeff's card that he was favourite for the open side forward Test spot against the French in the two game series played during the month of December. The first was at The Boulevard on 6th December which coincided with Bradford Northern's game against Widnes at Naughton Park, a game which Bradford won in great style 6–3 in a nail biter. The second Test was played at Stade Vélodrome De Marseille on 20th December when no games were played in this country.

Great Britain Versus France, First Test,
The Boulevard, Hull, 6 December 1981

The game at The Boulevard was unusual because there was an Australian referee in charge. Top whistler Greg Hartley was the man and he had a reputation of letting the game flow, just the thing to suit the French with their free flowing handling and their ability to release passes from impossible angles. Johnny Whiteley was the GB coach and Colin Hutton [Hull Kingston Rovers] the manager. The man in charge as coach of the French team was Louis Bonnery of Limoux.

Greg Hartley came in for some stick from the knowledgeable Hull spectators as he penalised both teams for forward passes, something the Boulevard experts had never seen before but this was a new innovation in Australia. Mr Hartley himself had been warned about the bitter games between France and Great Britain and the roughhouse tactics often used by both teams. During the game there was no argy-bargy. Things were so evenly tempered that it seemed like a Sunday stroll. The tame type of game suited the home side who were allowed to play a brand of rugby of which the Frenchmen had no answer. Henderson Gill, Wigan's new signing from Rochdale Hornets recorded a hat trick of tries. Des Drummond scored two and Steve Hartley and John Woods added further tries with Woods kicking seven goals and George Fairbairn one giving Great Britain a clear 37–nil victory. Steve Norton had an outstanding game and Jeff, relishing his new found ball handling job, had his supporting forwards running in every direction from his astute passes. Andy Gregory too had an excellent Great Britain debut. Jeff had a hand in the final try when he slipped a great pass which had Steve Norton racing clear from near his own try line. The Hull FC forward then found John Woods with a long pass and the Leigh flyer ran all of 70 yards to score.

France Versus Great Britain, Second Test, Stade Vélodrome, Marseilles, 20 December 1981

Bradford Northern played no games in the month of December so Jeff was pleased that he was selected for the return game in France on the 20th. Mr Greg Hartley, the Australian referee, was again in charge for this game in Marseilles. The French made wholesale changes from the side decimated by the in-form Brits at The Boulevard. If Mr Hartley thought the previous cross channel game was a walk in the park for him, this game must have seemed like a battlefield! This was Anglo-Gallic Rugby League warfare. It appeared that the French game plan was to pull the Anglos into a brawl with as many fights taking place on the pitch as there were passes of the ball. It was a spiteful, niggling game with two massive all in brawls, involving all 26 players, in the first half. The second brawl caused so much mayhem that Mr Hartley had to make a point so he dismissed Les Gorley in the 39th minute. Les was unfortunate as any of the other players could have walked.

John Woods gave the Brits the lead after six minutes with a penalty but never bothered the score board keeper again in the match and by half time the French led 9–2 through tries by Patrick Solal 2, a drop goal by Michel Laville and a conversion by Andre Perez. Greg Hartley was livid at half time and demanded a quick meeting with the two coaches, Johnny Whiteley and Louis Bonnery. He told them that he would give the players five minutes in the second half to show that they were prepared to play football and cut out the fighting. Marc Ambert and Joel Roosebrouck began to punch holes in the Brits' defence and Etienne Kaminski raced over for a try that sealed the win for France. Mr Hartley sent off Jacques Guigue for a high shot on Mick Burke three minutes from time and in the final seconds Christian Schicchitano raced over after a fine Roosebrouck break and Andre Perez converted both the Kaminski and Schicchitano tries to give the French a well deserved 19–2 win. It was a poor show by Great Britain who fell into a well laid trap of allowing the French to dictate the rise and fall of the game. The strong arm tactics certainly worked well for the French for, as we were fighting, they played some fast and entertaining football then when the Brits looked dangerous they ploughed in with the biff, bang, wallop. It was simple but effective.

League games resumed and Bradford recorded a good 25–12 win at Post Office Road, Featherstone against the Rovers. Next the tough Warrington side visited Odsal resulting in a hard fought 3 points all draw. Early February saw two bad results for Bradford losing 9–8 at home to Leigh and 15–10 to Hull Kingston Rovers at Craven Park. But it was that time of the year again when the Challenge Cup came around and as Jeff put it:

> Here it was again and surely taking into account the law of averages it had to be our time this season. Out of the hat came Bradford Northern versus Dewsbury, my old club.
>
> I had so many good memories from the old Crown Flatt that it was always a pleasure to play against them either home or away. We had to play them at Odsal and we thought we were good enough to progress into round two but Dewsbury could be a tough cup tie as they seemed to raise their game when the various cups were up for grabs.

On a wet Sunday afternoon this cup tie was played and went exactly the way Jeff thought it would. Bradford looked capable of running up a big score but could not shake off Dewsbury and it was a close call at the end, Bradford going through 14–12 in a tight finish. League wins against Barrow away 10–8 and Hull FC at Odsal by 14–8 put Bradford in good heart to take on Workington Town at Odsal in round two of the Challenge Cup. Town were accepted as one of the most difficult teams to be drawn against in any cup competition home or away. The old Cumberland tradition of an uncompromising, tough outfit who thrived on beating the big boys in cup football was still alive and kicking up there on the North West coast and again Bradford were made to fight every inch of the way to claim a 17–8 victory.

Castleford at Odsal were beaten 10–5 then Fulham at Craven Cottage were beaten 15–5 before the third round of the Challenge Cup. This crucial round was against the old enemy in cup football, Widnes. A real old fashioned cup fighting team with a great tradition, Widnes could field a side brim full of international players, Mick Burke, Eddie Cunningham, Eric Hughes, Keith Bentley, Andy Gregory, Mike O'Neill, Brian Lockwood, Mick Adams, Eric Prescott and Keith Elwell. This quarter final tie gave Bradford the advantage of a home draw. Jeff remembers:

> I had given up wondering and hoping for Wembley some time before but I had a feeling that we could go through in this tie if we did what we had been doing in previous games and if our key players all performed to their best abilities.

This was a close game throughout with both teams creating half chances but the covering defence on both sides was excellent. At the end of the 80 minutes the sides were locked in a breath taking draw at 8 points each. The replay was at Naughton Park the following Wednesday and the teams started where they had left off in the first game. No nonsense tackling, a bit of needle from the previous Saturday and the prospect of a place in the semi final put a great edge on this match and it was just as close as the first meeting of these clubs. But the old bogey of Jeff and Wembley struck again when the hooter sounded the end of the game and Widnes were in the lead 10–7. It was another heartbreaker for Jeff who shrugged his huge shoulders and said as usual, 'There is always next season!'

The next league game was Warrington at Wilderspool and Bradford really turned it on to gain a fabulous 21–nil win. Wigan at Central Park came next. I remember both the Wigan v Bradford fixtures that season as I was then the Wigan coach. The first league game between the two clubs had been in late September 1981 at Odsal which Bradford had won 12–5. The return fixture saw a real nail biter at Central Park with yet another 16–15 win for Bradford.

The run in to the play offs again saw Bradford finish the league season with a flourish winning six of the seven games in April. Their one defeat was at Headingley against Leeds 22–6. The run of wins included Featherstone Rovers at home 24–17, Leeds at home 20–10, Wakefield Trinity at home 28–7, York at home 22–15, York away 30–19 and Fulham at Odsal 8–5 gave Bradford an away championship play off game at Craven Park to take on Hull Kingston Rovers. This proved to be a game too far and The Robins were successful with a 17–8 win. But this final game of the season ended in controversy. The 9 points difference in scores failed to show just how close the game actually was and as the passages of play took Bradford Northern up field to launch another attack, Jeff was held in a treble tackle by the Hull Kingston Rovers defence and one or two blows were struck.

Now Bradford had not had the best of calls from the referee and he again whistled and gave a penalty to Hull Kingston Rovers accusing Jeff of being the aggressor. Jeff appealed against the decision saying that he was carrying the ball and defending his face with the other hand and arm. But the referee would not listen and Jeff, in his rage, threw the ball at the referee, Mr Robin Whitfield and hit the official on the head. The referee ordered Jeff from the field but Jeff was in a distressed condition with his jersey almost pulled off and his shoulder pads almost hanging off him. Mr Whitfield insisted that Jeff was motioning his team mates to follow him from the field but later it was accepted that he was only rearranging his playing kit. Moving his shoulders and arms in a flaying motion to straighten up his pads and ease his jersey into position, the Bradford players had moved in to support their much respected prop. Someone on the Bradford side must have said, 'Well if he's sending Jeff off we're going as well,' and as Jeff walked off the field so did the remainder of the Bradford team.

It was a bizarre end to the season and caused a commotion at the RFL HQ. The result stood and Jeff was not allowed to attend the inquest into how and what actually happened. Instead he was represented at this meeting by the Rugby League Players union but was suspended for six matches in one of the most unfair hearings for many years. In the immediate close season the suspension was reduced by one match to five matches.

* * * * *

The 1982–83 season appeared to have been Jeff's farewell period in international Rugby League. There was a whole catalogue of logical reasons as to why Jeff had doubts about his future playing for Great Britain. He was 33 years old and had already played for so long, he took his share of the blame for the defeat against the French in Marseilles and there had been his most unusual reaction in the Hull Kingston Rovers game at the end of last season. But he served his sentence and on resuming in the front row his form was as good as ever. His come back game was against the tough Workington Town up at Derwent Park in a bone hard 5 points all draw. The team had beaten Hull Kingston Rovers 15–14 at Odsal and York again at Odsal in the Yorkshire Cup whilst Jeff was suspended but he was clear to play in the 11–nil win at Post Office Road, Featherstone in the County Cup semi final. This set up a final tie of Bradford against Hull FC at Headingley on Saturday 2nd October.

Bradford had to play a league game against Hull FC first at Odsal and the Airlie Birds won a hard fought contest 6–nil. Another loss, this time to Warrington at Wilderspool 15–6, was not the ideal preparation for the Yorkshire Cup final which was next on the agenda. Since way back in 1972–73, when Jeff first tasted the Big Stage of professional Rugby League, he seldom had a period of his career when there was nothing happening. His original visit to Australia to play at Cronulla, his selection at various international levels, his County experience as a regular Yorkshire player, his tour as a Lion, his captaincy of his County and his country, his transfer to Bradford Northern and in fact his life in football had been one exciting and breathtaking ride. The shadow of Wembley hung over him and during the many years he'd played at this high level, this was always going to be the year! The new challenge this particular weekend was to possess a Yorkshire Cup winners medal for the first time in his 11 years in the top flight of the game.

Bradford Northern Versus Hull FC, Yorkshire Cup Final, Headingley, Leeds, 2 October 1982

The scene was set on this cool October afternoon and the superb Headingley ground was the ideal setting. The industrious and superb footballer Alan Redfearn had been injured in the league game at Featherstone and unfortunately the injury had not responded to treatment. Consequently Bradford went into the final with a re-arranged back division. Dean Carroll moved from stand off to scrum half and Keith Whiteman played at stand off half. The loss of Alan Redfearn was a body blow to Bradford and his skill as a game controller, a fearless defender and a crucial try poacher would be sadly missed. Hull FC had brought in some superb players including Gary Kemble, David Topliss and Trevor Skerrett as they attempted a return to the great days at The Boulevard.

The outcome of the game was disappointing for Jeff and his team mates. Bradford were beaten by tries by Steve Evans, Paul Prendiville and Paul Rose (2) and two Lee Crooks goals plus two drop goals giving Hull FC 18 points against Bradford's 7 points made up by a Keith Whiteman try and a Dean Carroll goal and two drop goals. The strength of the Hull FC club at this time can be seen in the consecutive Yorkshire Cup finals they were involved in. Including this final against Bradford the Airlie Birds appeared in four out of a possible five in the mid 1980s.

Bradford's confidence seemed to wane a wee bit immediately after this County Cup final and the team recorded only two wins out of the next seven games. Even taking into account the fact that one of the defeats was a creditable one against the 'Invincible' Australian 1982 touring side by 13–6, the ratio of defeats was unacceptable at Odsal. The two wins in this awkward period were against Leigh away by 23–15 and Featherstone Rovers away by 17–5. The other defeats were against Wigan away 13–4, Hull Kingston Rovers at Odsal 5–3, Widnes away 20–9, Hull Kingston Rovers away 11–5 and the Aussie tourists.

The selectors did not even consider Jeff's retirement from the international scene as his club form, despite the club's run of poor results, had been excellent.

8

A DISASTROUS TEST

The first Test of this series was played on 30th October at Boothferry Park, the home of Hull City FC. The Australians had come on this tour unannounced. No one had any idea just how good they were and the squad included many unknown players. The Great Britain coach was John Whiteley the former world class loose forward who had played for Hull FC. John had coached a successful tour in 1970 and was the last British coach to win the Ashes series with Frank Myler as his captain.

All at the Rugby Football League totally underestimated this touring side and the new internationals they brought over produced shock waves within our game from which we never recovered. They were the same old Aussie type of player, big and powerful but they played the game at breakneck speed with tremendously skilful handling, tackling and kicking that we had never seen before. We went into the series with the same mental and physical attitude that we had since the 1950s and the Aussies were light years ahead of us. It was not the fault of any coach or player, it was the fault of the Rugby Football League who had allowed the Australian coaching scheme to race ahead trying out new innovations in play and new defensive drills in training techniques that left us gasping.

The innovator of the new approach to conditioning which put the onus on defence was the famous coaching Guru Jack Gibson who would go over to his friend's home in the USA and watch a grid iron team work out. Jack took in aspects he considered useful for our game. The whole Sydney league used these modern techniques every day in games. They re-wrote the coaching manual and this 1982 touring squad were the results of hours of perfect practice. Jeff and his Great Britain mates were about to be led onto the sacrificial altar in front of almost 30,000 spectators.

Australia Versus Great Britain, First Test, Boothferry Park, Hull, 30 October 1982

The Australians ignored the biff and played some unbelievable football, although at half time the Brits were within striking distance, only 10–4 behind. But the ominous signs were on the wall when Craig Young and Wayne Pearce sliced through the home defence and fed the big centre Mal Meninga who was challenged by one of the strongest centres in the British game, Les Dyl. Meninga simply swatted Les away with a mighty handoff and appeared to almost ignore his tackle as he strode to the posts for a try which took the wind out of not only our Test team but also the game in general in this country. Our strongest centre simply skittled aside. The powerful Les Boyd then steam rolled his way through three tacklers. Two Meninga goals against two goals from Lee Crooks gave the misleading feeling that Great Britain could pull this one back. Jeff remembers:

I walked off the pitch at half time thinking, 'these Aussies have come on a bit since I played out there but we'll click again in the second half and catch them up'. But to be fair we couldn't get within yards of them when they turned it on and we had some hard lads out there make no mistake. Some of their support play was excellent and when the ball reached the super fast Boustead and the big, strong Eric Grothe we had no answers.

In Robert Gate's book *100 years of Test Matches*, the historian recalls that 'the second half was an exhilarating exhibition of the best things in Rugby League by Australia but an embarrassment for Britain's. Possibly this result was worse than the defeat at Swinton in 1963 in the 50–12 massacre'.

The Aussies scored six tries in the second 40 minutes through Eric Grothe, a wonderful wingman's try, Kerry Boustead, Brett Kenny, Ray Price and Rod Reddy with Meninga kicking another six goals. The result of 40–4 sent shock waves reaching even into the Rugby Football League's boardroom.

The day after the drubbing in the Test match Jeff turned out for Bradford Northern at Hilton Park, Leigh and wore the number 15 jersey as one of Northern's subs. He was called into duty and scored one of Bradford's tries in the 23–15 win. Jeff wanted to play for his club as he knew that his presence on the field would be an asset to Northern as they needed as many wins as possible to make up for the run of recent defeats. The following week Bradford Northern played the Aussie tourists at Odsal. Jeff led the Bradford pack in fine style and the Odsal crowd cheered their players off at the end for the Bradford team had played their hearts out to take the Aussies all the way in a tremendous effort to hold the rampant tourists to 13–6. Featherstone Rovers were beaten 17–5 at Odsal but the old antagonists Hull Kingston Rovers beat Bradford at Craven Park 11–5. Jeff did not play in this game as the day before he had represented Great Britain in the second Test against Australia at Central Park, Wigan. The Test selectors were in a spin.

Australia Versus Great Britain, Second Test, Central Park, Wigan, 20 November 1982

The horrific result at Boothferry Park had shocked them to the core. In an effort to evade another heavy defeat Great Britain made ten changes to the 15 man team. The five remaining from the first Test were Des Drummond, Jeff Grayshon, Trevor Skerrett, Ken Kelly and John Woods. One positional change was Ken Kelly coming off the subs bench to replace John Woods who reverted to the bench. Jeff was made captain as the selectors wanted to draw on his experience to try and stop the rot. The Aussies left their winning 13 alone and made two changes on the subs' bench, Steve Ella and John Muggleton giving way to Wally Lewis and Ray Brown. Wally Lewis was the original first choice stand off but such was the form of Brett Kenny in the run up to the first Test that Wally had to wait in the wings for his chance for a Test run on this tour. This showed the strength of the Aussies.

The Kangaroos were again in brilliant form but the Great Britain defence was a touch better than at Hull. The Lions held their own again for the first 20 minutes but when the Aussies opened up, the home defence was swept away and even the sending off of Les Boyd on 34 minutes made little difference. Keith Mumby kicked three first half penalties but the Aussies scored three super tries as Ray Price, Peter Sterling and Eric Grothe all crossed and Mal Meninga kicked three goals to go in at half time ahead 15–6.

The 12 Australians increased their lead with tries by Meninga and Steve Rogers with Meninga adding three further goals. A lingering memory of this game is that the crowd of 23,216 stood to applaud the 25 yard wide spin pass by Wally Lewis that sent in Mal Meninga for his try. Then as the game came to a close a passing move involving all 12 Australian players had the crowd on their feet again cheering and applauding such breathtaking skills. Although well beaten again, two or three Lions could hold their heads up, one being Jeff who belied his 33 years against a blistering Aussie attack with some sound defence around the play the ball.

After the two heavy defeats and losing the Ashes again the selectors decided to look for some new blood for the tour of Australia and New Zealand in 1984. This meant Jeff, and several others, were not selected for the final Test eight days later. This was easier said than done. There were some good young backs on the horizon but not many Test level forwards. Nevertheless Jeff was turning in some terrific performances for his club and as long as this continued that was all that mattered.

It was the time of year for the John Player Trophy to begin and Bradford had to travel the short distance to Lawkholme Lane to take on Keighley. Northern went through to round two with an 18–0 win. Round two saw a clash at Odsal against the side who beat them in the County Cup final, Hull FC. In a tough nail biter Bradford held out against this purpose bought side to draw 12 points all and replay the following Wednesday at The Boulevard. Bradford did it the hard way by winning at Hull FC 10–8 in another real blood and guts game. Jeff remembers:

> I recall feeling that it was about time we had a bit of luck with a home draw in the hardest round of any cup competition. The draw took us to the toughest place in the game, Widnes at Naughton Park! The Hull FC games and this Widnes tie were very similar in content. Both were tight, hard tussles with forward play the order of the day. I managed a close in try at Widnes but at home the Chemics were a handful and despite a great effort by all the lads we went out of the John Player Trophy by 16–10.

Over Christmas Bradford's fixtures were Halifax at Thrum Hall on Boxing Day and again Bradford played Halifax two days later at Odsal. On 2 January, Bradford played Castleford at Wheldon Road. Keith Mumby received an injury at Leigh the day after the second Test and missed 14 games for Bradford in this season. John Green deputised and Bradford received the same super performances from the youngster who played exceedingly well. Halifax produced a real Boxing Day fighting display to beat Bradford 10–2. In the return match at Odsal, Bradford won 10–6. Bradford played extremely well against Castleford to return home 15–13 winners. Jeff felt that:

> My favourite time of the season was fast approaching, that, of course, was the Challenge Cup rounds which began in February. We were going okay at home but found travelling to games a bit inconsistent, for instance we had good wins against Barrow, Carlisle and Leigh but failed against Oldham and Hull FC away. One game that got away from us was a 4–nil defeat at Odsal by Wigan. This was one we should have won comfortably but we threw away several great chances to score tries and paid the penalty. The Challenge Cup first round draw gave us York at Odsal which we managed to win 23–5. Barrow beat us up at Craven Park 10–5 but the following week we travelled down to London to play Fulham RLFC. They gave us a really tough game and we were fortunate to come away with an 11–4 win that took us into round three, the crucial round.
>
> The whole team clustered around the radio to hear the draw 'Workington Town will play Bradford Northern,' said the reporter. This was a difficult game to win especially in the Challenge Cup. But we went up with confidence in ourselves and were highly satisfied with our 17–nil win.

Bradford were into yet another semi final and Jeff's old feelings that this could be the year came flooding back. Northern had drawn those tough cup fighters Featherstone Rovers. They had played Featherstone twice already this season, in the Yorkshire Cup at Post Office Road (winning 11–nil) and in the league game at Odsal (beating them 17–5). But they also knew that those results meant nothing and playing them in the final game of the season away would be meaningless if they slipped up in the big cup tie. Bradford beat Warrington at Wilderspool 23–14 on the weekend between the third round and the semi final and the team approached the semi in great heart. The clubs left in the cup were Bradford, Featherstone, Hull FC and Castleford. Jeff continues:

> Our semi was drawn to be played at Headingley, the other at Elland Road. Our game attracted less than 11,000 spectators, a disappointing gate considering the prestige the semi finals usually generate. Featherstone went for the players who had seen them through to the semi, Barker; Marsden, Quinn, Gilbert, Kellett; Banks, Hudson; Gibbins, Handscombe, Hankins, Hobbs, Slatter and Peter Smith with the subs Lyman and Siddall. Peter Fox went into the game with us all ready, or so we thought. Our side was Mumby; Smith, Hanley, Davies, Whiteman; Hale, Redfearn; myself, Noble, Van Bellen, Jackson, Idle and Rathbone with the subs Jasiewicz and Carroll. Again the worst happened as we could not get on top of a grand side full of local lads. For one short period I thought 'We can win this', but we had to give credit for how Featherstone played that afternoon and for me the dream had faded again.

Featherstone Rovers went on to lift the cup at Wembley with another great performance against a strong Hull FC.

Another disappointing defeat at Odsal by Widnes followed the semi final but Bradford dropped only one point in the final six games in this season. A draw against Leeds at Headingley, 5 points each, then five wins on the trot, Leeds at Odsal 27–6, St Helens 13–6 at Knowsley Road, Workington Town at Odsal,

Carlisle away 55–3 and Featherstone Rovers away 24–13. It had been another setback for a Wembley trip. Yet again Jeff was on the losing side in the Challenge Cup semi final and again had been in the Bradford side beaten by Hull FC in the County Cup final. Now 34 years old and having been around the block a time or two Jeff never once considered it time to close the book. Considering the knocks he had taken and the horrendous knee injury he'd suffered in Australia Jeff felt that he could go on. Sure he had lost pace, which had been one of his strong suits, but his strength and experience would see him through in the style that Peter Fox wanted him to play. Jeff was still a big man and his ability to stand in the tackle and deliver spot on passes was a feature of prop forward play in those days. Jeff was looking forward to the next season with as much enthusiasm as any of the youngsters recently signed on for Bradford.

* * * * *

The writer's connection with Jeff goes back quite a few years as I first met him in 1972 when I was the assistant coach at Dewsbury. It was always good meeting up with Jeff as I moved around in the coaching circuit. I mention this because in the 1983–84 season, I was coaching at the Leeds club and we played Bradford Northern four times that term. But Bradford's season began brightly enough, getting that long trip to Whitehaven out of the way in the early season light nights. In fact it was the first game of the new season and it was good to get a comfortable 45–4 win for a change. Hull Kingston Rovers were beaten in the Yorkshire Cup 25–22 a week after Bradford had registered a fine win over Oldham at the Watersheddings. Wigan were beaten at Central Park (24–16) but then Bradford were beaten at Odsal by Castleford (12–8) in round two of the County Cup. Jeff and the team bounced back by winning three on the trot at home against St Helens (14–10), at Leigh (24–0) and against Salford at Odsal (38–14). Hull KR, Bradford's bogey team, beat them in the return against 16–14, Jeff recalled:

> We just could not get regular results against Hull Kingston. We would be equal to them throughout the game then we would lose concentration for a split second and they would score tries that took the game away from us. Other teams that seemed to have a jinx on us were Widnes and on occasion, Castleford.

Jeff also mentioned that of all the tough props he played against, the one who gave him the most trouble in the set scrums and who caught him more than once with the crash tackle (his party piece), was Dennis Boyd of Wigan and Leigh.

> Dennis would come into you at an angle, usually as you were looking to take a pass from your right, Dennis would arrive from your left and hit you like a torpedo in the ribs. I've had the wind knocked out of me by him on many an occasion. St Helens were another side who could clean you out in a few minutes if you let them run. You would be in control of the game then bang, bang, bang, they could hit you from anywhere on the field and within minutes there was no way back.

That is exactly what Saints did to Bradford at Knowsley Road. They hit Bradford with a blitz to beat them 29 –14.

Another bogey team, Featherstone Rovers, were beaten 30–10 and a fine win at home to Fulham by 21–2 put Bradford in good spirits to tackle their old foes Widnes in the first round of the John Player Trophy at Naughton Park. This game was possibly the most unusual game of Rugby League ever played. At the final whistle the score was Widnes 2 Bradford Northern 1. Ever since the devaluation of the drop goal to one point this score was a possibility.

Bradford went on to beat Salford away (14–12), Wakefield

Trinity at home (20–15), Warrington away (13–11) and Fulham away (21–2) and then Widnes arrived at Odsal to wallop Bradford 24–14. Castleford took a point at Odsal on New Year's Day in a 2 points all draw and Hull FC proved too strong for Bradford with a 16–8 win at The Boulevard. As the season drew on, the Challenge Cup suddenly dawned and we were in February, the month of the first round ties. Bradford had drawn Featherstone Rovers at Odsal but the week before Hull Kingston Rovers came to Bradford and were soundly beaten 20–nil with Jeff turning the clock back with a two try performance. Featherstone were tumbled out of the cup as Bradford rattled up a 20–4 winning result and Hunslet were drawn away to play at the Elland Road ground in round two. Castleford recorded a big score in the league against Northern at Wheldon Road in a 29–6 win. The brave Hunslet were no match for Bradford in the cup and went down by a score of 17–7 with Bradford drawing Leeds away in the third round. Defeats by Wigan at Odsal (15–6), Jeff scoring Bradford's try, and Oldham at the Watersheddings (10–4), set the scene for a classic cup tie at Headingley on 11 March 1983.

On a brilliantly sunny afternoon Bradford Northern fielded Keith Mumby, David Smith, Steve Parrish, Gary Hale, Keith Whiteman; Dean Carroll, Andy Robinson; Jeff Grayshon, Brian Noble, Gary Van Bellen, Alan Rathbone, Dick Jasiewcz and Sheldon, the subs were, Mark Fleming and Graham Idle. The Leeds side I selected included Ian Wilkinson: Paul Prendiville, David Creasser, Dean Bell, Neil Hague; John Holmes, Steve Martin; Keith Rayne, David Ward, Kevin Rayne, Gary Moorby, Mark Laurie and Terry Webb, the subs were Kevin Dick and Trevor Clark. The issue looked all over as this game approached the final three minutes. Bradford seemed to have beaten Leeds and were on their way to yet another semi final.

Alan Rathbone had stormed over for an early try and Steve Parrish converted then kicked a couple of penalty goals to give Bradford a 10–nil lead at half time. Suddenly, early in the second half, Leeds were back in the game as David Creasser gave the team a start with a long range penalty goal, then the great footballer Steve Martin, the Aussie half back, scored one of his special tries with David Creasser converting making the score 10–8 to Northern. The clock was ticking away but Leeds seemed to be getting on top. Jeff was holding the Bradford pack together, keeping the ball tight amongst his excellent pack with some terrific late passes that stretched the defence. A Parrish penalty goal pushed Northern out to a 12–8 advantage and Dean Carroll struck a magnificent drop goal to seemingly, at 13–8, put the semi final next round out of Leeds' grasp.

Nearing the end of the game, Ian Wilkinson used his strength to force his way over in the corner, 13–12 with only two minutes to play. From the kick off the Leeds forwards took play to the half way line and a combined Australian move by Terry Webb and Mark Laurie made a final 25 yards on the last tackle in the set. Neil Hague had supported Mark Laurie's surge and was at acting half back as the 80 minutes was up. Neil picked up the ball, threw a dummy pass and swivelled on his left leg to take a snap drop at goal. The Headingley ground erupted as the ball turned sweetly between the posts and over the cross bar to take the game to 13 points apiece. There was a period of two minutes' injury time so all Leeds had to do was catch the ball, run out the five tackles and kick the ball out of the ground! From the kick off Leeds lost the ball. This meant there was a final scrum with time only for two tackles at most. Bradford won the ball at the scrum and Andy Robinson went for a beak to the open side of the field and was held about 35 yards out in mid field. It was the final tackle of the game and

Dean Carroll called for the ball and hit a good drop at goal only to see the ball fade away to the right. The hooter sounded to give Leeds the right to go to Odsal the following Wednesday evening for the replay.

In those days coaches got up to all sorts of sneaky tricks to attempt to gain the advantage. As coach at Leeds I found myself in a dilemma at the Sunday morning fitness roll call at Headingley. My captain David Ward had suffered a back spasm and was unfit and the influential Terry Webb had pulled a calf muscle. Not wanting to tip my hand to Peter Fox I informed the *Yorkshire Evening Post* that John Holmes would not be fit for the replay. I knew that all the Bradford players rated John highly as a player so to camouflage the loss of David Ward and Terry Webb I focused the attention on John Holmes.

It was rather comical when we arrived at Odsal for we disguised John and had him help carry the kit from the bus to the dressing rooms. Much to Bradford's surprise, John was on the pitch at the kick off. To say this game was close would be an understatement. Again Bradford looked like overall winners for most of the game but could not collect the required points to ever feel safe. Both sides scored two tries, Noble and Carroll for Northern and Prendiville and Squire for Leeds but whereas Steve Parrish could only muster one goal, David Creasser kicked two for Leeds. There was a scare in the final seconds as Bradford were awarded a penalty and Dean Carroll picked up the ball and placed in for a kick at goal. Young Parrish had missed a couple of kickable shots and Dean must have considered the distance too far for the young centre. He struck the ball well but, as at Headingley, it drifted wide of the posts and Leeds were through with a 12–10 victory.

This was another huge disappointment for Jeff who by now

must have thought that the gods did not intend him walking out at Wembley. By now Bradford could have won the cup tie twice! Kevin Squire's try at Odsal in the final few minutes was hotly disputed by both the home players and fans as Kevin burrowed over from a play the ball less than a yard from the try line. That made the score 10 points all and David Creasser rubbed it in with a superb touchline conversion.

'There's always next season,' said Jeff philosophically repeating something he had said for so long. Jeff missed two of the last three games of that season, returning for the play off game at The Boulevard against Hull FC where Northern were unceremoniously removed from the competition with a score of Hull FC 42 Bradford Northern 12.

In the 1984–85 season, which turned out to be Jeff's last season with Peter Fox at Odsal, he missed only three games. Despite being 35 years old, his fitness, experience and dedication to the game was there for all to see in his playing statistics. Although not scoring as many tries as in years gone by he still knew the way to the line as he registered tries against Hunslet and Wigan, both at Odsal. This too was Jeff's last full season in his first spell for the Bradford Club. He had seen many good players serve Bradford Northern, for example Jimmy Thompson, Colin Forsyth, Alan Redfearn, David Redfearn who played on after Jeff moved away, Denis Trotter, Nigel Stephenson, Neil Fox, Tony Fisher, Geoff Clarkson, Len Casey, David Barends, Henderson Gill, Ian Van Bellen, Keith Bridges, Bob Haigh, Les Gant and many others. At the season's start he was playing as well as ever and relished the new term as it might have brought that yearned for Wembley trip. A set back in the first game was an away defeat to Hull Kingston Rovers 34–6. The next two excellent wins at Wigan (9–2) and Featherstone Rovers at Odsal (28–8) were followed by the first round of the old Yorkshire Cup and a resounding win over Wakefield Trinity at Belle Vue (30–nil). Next Bradford beat Castleford at Odsal 20–10.

The second round of the County Cup brought together the old antagonists Bradford and Leeds. A good crowd assembled at Odsal and witnessed a real tough cup tie by two in-form sides. Leeds were coming off a narrow home defeat by Oldham, but were strengthened by the return of Jeff's old touring mate David Ward. Gary Moorby scored the Leeds try in their 10–4 victory with David Creasser kicking two goals and Kevin Dick and David Ward dropping a goal each. Bradford's points came from two Ellery Hanley penalty goals. The big crowd were not disappointed as the football served up was exciting and there was not much between the teams meaning the challenges in defence were ferocious, just as a cup tie should be.

So Bradford were out of the County Cup. Jeff and his mates continued gaining good results in the league games. Saints were the next opponents for Bradford at Odsal and Northern resumed winning ways with a stunning 30–10 win. Now approaching the start of the John Player Trophy competition Bradford tuned up with wins against Hunslet at home 72–12 and Widnes at home 17–10 but they lost two games to the tough Workington Town away by 5–3 and to Oldham 23–14 at Odsal. Bradford negotiated the long trip to Carlisle without problems and achieved a 26–8 win to go through to the next round. A good win in the league against Leigh at Hilton Park 30–28 kept things bubbling before round two of the John Player, which Jeff missed, brought Swinton to Odsal and with it a sound 22–1 victory. Then the strange nature of cup football was seen in its glory as Bradford played St Helens in the league, away, and Bradford lost heavily, for them, 28–6. Seven days later the visitors to Odsal in round three of the John Player Trophy were St Helens! This was a difficult tie. Saints had the mighty Australian Mal Meninga in their centres and a wealth of international players and future international players throughout the side, and in a game that could have gone either way, at the final whistle the score was 12 points all. Tries in the first half to David Smith and Steve McGowan and one goal from Steve Parrish against two tries by Barrie Ledger and Peter Gorley gave Northern a 10–8 advantage and a Steve Parrish goal and two goals for Saints by Sean Day gave the draw at full time. Jeff says:

> This was a tough cup tie and we had all the chances in the world to win it but Saints held out and they were full of confidence about entertaining us at their ground in the replay. The crowd of over 9,000 enjoyed the football and the bust-ups and were royally entertained for 80 minutes.

The replay on the Wednesday saw Saints make one change in the starting team, Roy Haggerty in the centre for the injured Shaun Allen and Johnny Smith came onto the subs bench for Haggerty. For Bradford Alan Rathbone was back in at loose forward for the injured Mark Fleming and Richard Davies took Alan Rathbone's sub spot. The result of the replay was a similar one to the league game only 10 days before with Saints winning by 24–10. Tries for Saints were scored by Sean Day, Neil Holding (2) and Harry Pinner with Day landing four goals. Bradford's replied with tries by David Smith and Ellery Hanley and one goal from Steve Parrish.

Cup football in those days had that strange nature of throwing up ties which strained every player on your register's stamina. To play a team like the one Saints fielded really did drain one's physical recourses and to play such games three times in 10 days showed the strength of character those players had. So exhausted were the players that the following game at Elland Road against Hunslet, a team Bradford had beaten only seven weeks ago 72–12, ended in a 12 all draw!

Bradford defeated Workington Town 26–16 and Barrow 28–12 both at Odsal but lost to Halifax at Thrum Hall 26–8 and Castleford at Wheldon Road 16–2 on New Year's Day. Jeff missed this particular game because of a bad back. They also lost to Oldham at the Watersheddings 16–14 and Warrington at Wilderspool 26–14 before they had a breather against Southend Invictor at Odsal in the first round of the Challenge Cup. They won this game 50–18 which brought Wakefield Trinity to Odsal in round two. Trinity were beaten 13–2 and revenge was taken against Warrington with a fine 22–4 win at Odsal.

The dreaded third round of the Challenge Cup came next and Bradford were lucky enough to get another home tie against a revived Wigan side who came to Odsal with a strong team. The jinx struck again as Wigan went through to the semi finals with a 7–6 win. Again Jeff was disappointed. The Wembley dream was blown away again. But it was business as usual for the ultimate professional Jeff Grayshon with a trip up to Barrow and a grand 24–20 win at Craven Park. Widnes beat Bradford at Naughton Park 34–18 but then came three great wins, Leigh at home 44–16, Wigan at home with an unbelievable score of 36–6 and a magnificent win at Headingley where Leeds were beaten 24–14.

The return game against Leeds was played the following Wednesday at Odsal which Leeds won 12–11. There then followed three poor results for Bradford, all away, Featherstone Rovers lost 25–10, Hull FC lost 24–18 and Hull Kingston Rovers lost 26–12 before the final two league games of the season brought smiles back to Northern supporters with two fine wins against Halifax 16–3 and a revenge win over Hull FC both at Odsal. The play offs took Bradford to Craven Park to play Hull Kingston Rovers where Bradford's season ended with a 42–18 defeat.

* * * * *

In early November 1984 the writer was invited to become the Great Britain coach. I was allowed to remain the Leeds coach until February 1985 and then I was not allowed to coach any professional club. My final game as the Leeds coach was a win at Widnes on 3rd February. Malcolm Clift an Australian coach took over from me until the end of the season. During the close season of 1984–85 Peter Fox left Odsal to take my old job at Headingley. Jeff was now 36 years old and unbelievably playing as well as ever but it was understandable that Jeff was at a loss after his friend and mentor Peter Fox left Bradford.

Great Britain Versus France, Limoux, 1 June 1985

The 1984 tour of Australia had ended with Great Britain beaten in all six Tests against the Aussies and Kiwis. The Aussies were an awesome set as we had seen in 1982 and the Kiwis were on the move and were almost as good as the Aussies. My job was to find new blood for our national side and in my first international game Great Britain beat the French 50–4. In the return game in Perpignan the inexperienced young GB side were beaten 24–16 and the French thought they saw a window from which they could gain complete revenge for the 0 point job we did on them earlier. They also possibly underestimated the good young potential players that I hadn't used in the Perpignan game. So the French authorities issued a challenge to us to play the French for a memorial cup in honour of two

French Rugby League journalists who had recently died in a motor accident. Our Rugby Football League accepted the challenge and instructed me to select a team to play this game on 1 June 1985 in the beautiful town of Limoux in the South of France.

Several of the young players I had pencilled in for the Test matches in the forthcoming Kiwi Tests were playing in Australia so I could give a chance to the other players knocking on the international door. But I needed an on field minder for these young players and the man I wanted was Jeff Grayshon, if he still had the ambition and enthusiasm to do the job for me. I contacted Jeff and he was delighted. This game did not count as an official international match so does not appear in any list of international appearances. The Great Britain side contained 17 players against the 19 available to the French. The starting 13 contained some interesting selections that were, at that time, very much in the full international window. The British lads were up for it and set about this tough French side with gusto.

Any Anglo-French game is never without a bit of hey-lads-hey and there were several pitched battles and one particularly big brawl between almost every player on the field. Jeff laughs about it now as he recalls:

A scrum broke up and big Max Chantal swung a haymaker at me. It missed, thank goodness, so I dabbed him on the chin and down he went. Immediately the whole French pack turned on me and our lads came in at the same time. I was taking on the hooker Bernabe when someone called out, 'Behind you Jeff!' and I felt a punch on the eyebrow. I turned to see the bloke off and came face to face with the smallest, fastest man on the field, Didier Couston. When he saw that his punch had not had the effect he wanted he must have noticed the expression on my face and turned, heading for pastures greener. I gave chase and the sight of me trying to catch this whippet brought howls of laughter from the lads, some of whom were still fighting.

But between the fighting we were doing all the scoring with Ellery Hanley in imperious mood, showing his world class rating with five glorious tries.

Joe Lydon romped over for a couple of tries and was followed across the whitewash by David Heron and Henderson Gill. David Creasser landed five goals to give us a great revenge win for the 46–8 defeat in Perpignan, Hugues Ratier and Didier Couston scored tries for France and Luc Mendez kicked one goal.

Jeff returned to Odsal but found things different after his old friend Peter Fox departed. Jeff's old touring mate, John Woods, had been signed from Leigh and Jeff trained hard in readiness for the new season. Jeff played in the opening game at Warrington where The Wire inflicted a heavy defeat on them by 32–7. Jeff hurt his back, an old injury, and missed seven games and whilst off asked Bradford Northern for a release or to go onto the transfer list. The club said they would think about it but Jeff knew that if he stopped playing for them the club would never release him, so when fit again he resumed his career at Odsal. Proving his fitness, he was in the Northern team that lost to Dewsbury 10–8 at Odsal and who beat Swinton 48–20 at Odsal. Now the New Zealand tourists were over here to play the 1985 Test series and had come with a great reputation boasting several players considered to be the best in the world at that time and at least the equal of the Australians.

On 23rd October the new Yorkshire coach, Peter Fox, announced his side to play the Kiwis at Odsal in the regular touring fixture against the County sides. The Kiwis fielded a weakened side with the first test in mind but all the tourists were considered to be the best 26 players in New Zealand. Yorkshire won handsomely 18–8 and scored tries through Carl

Gibson, Ellery Hanley and Andy Goodway and two Deryck Fox goals and a drop goal each to Ellery Hanley and Gary Schofield. New Zealand replied with a Mark Elia try and two goals by Joe Roparti and Owen Wright.

Great Britain Versus New Zealand, Second Test, Central Park, Wigan, 2 November 1985

Jeff had played his final game for Bradford in this spell at the club. He was having treatment for the ongoing back problem and after the Yorkshire game in which he had a storming match, his back stiffened again and he had intensive treatment from a Leeds consultant.

After the first Test played on 19th October at Leeds, I had selected Lee Crooks of Hull FC to play at open side prop. Lee was injured between the first and second Test and I needed a big prop who knew Test football. At the time, Great Britain had a shortage of Test class players and the position of open side prop forwards was particularly short of potential players. We had narrowly lost that first Test and had to win the second at Central Park, Wigan to stay in the series. I phoned Jeff and asked if he would do a job for us against the Kiwis. He didn't hesitate for a second and accepted my invitation to play. Also in the 15 man squad for this game was Shaun Edwards of Wigan who was the then youngest player for Great Britain at age 17. The introduction of Jeff also gave us the oldest player ever to play for Great Britain at almost 37.

The full squad of 17 players moved into camp at the Shaw Hill leisure complex near Chorley. We prepared very well and on that afternoon of 2 November 1985 we beat the Kiwis 25–8. Jeff Grayshon's contribution to the performance was outstanding both on the field and off it. His steadying influence in the dressing room before the game and at half time had a huge effect both in the way the team played and also in the cool way the side faced up to the New Zealanders' 'in your face' style. The player who stole the show by making headlines in the press was Gary Schofield who scored four scintillating tries adding to the four goals by Joe Lydon and a Harry Pinner drop goal. For the well beaten Kiwis Dean Bell scored a try and Olsen Filipaina kicked two goals. The other big news stories that broke besides Gary's four tries, was that both Shaun Edwards and Jeff were together on the playing field giving that 'youngest and oldest player' official record status. Jeff then signed for Leeds whilst in the Test camp at Chorley.

Great Britain Versus New Zealand, Third Test, Elland Road, Leeds, 9 November 1985

Jeff returned to club training not at Odsal, as he had done so many times, but to Headingley to rejoin his old friend Peter Fox but not before he had finished his pre Test camp at Shaw Hill for the third, final and crucial Test match. The match was played in Leeds again but this time at Elland Road, the home of Leeds United. Tony Myler was declared unfit the day before the game so Ellery Hanley moved to stand off half and young Shaun Edwards took Ellery's place in the centre. Chris Arkwright of St Helens came onto the subs bench for Shaun and Lee Crooks was back after injury to fill in the sub forward spot. This was an old fashioned Test match with the old fashioned biff! Only one try was scored in the game which was hotly disputed by all the British players in the immediate area of the touchdown as Kiwi skipper Mark Graham appeared to lose the ball as he plunged over. But Mr Gomersall said 'Try!' and Dane Sorenson added the conversion.

New Zealand had done their homework and Kurt Sorenson knocked out Andy Goodway with a horrific head high tackle in the 23rd minute. Lee Crooks entered the field and eventually won the man of the match award. David Watkinson and Wayne Wallace were having a Test match of their own battling at almost every scrum. So six points down after Mark Graham's score on 32 minutes, it was left to Lee Crooks to get us cracking with his first penalty goal on 48 minutes then the big forward landed another on 56 minutes as the Kiwis continued using strong arm tactics intended to put us off. An all-in brawl started at a scrum on in the 63rd minute and Mr Gomersall allowed advantage to Great Britain as we were on a strong attack and three play the balls were carried out whilst all the forwards were fighting fiercely. When order was restored the referee sent Jeff and Kurt Sorenson to the sin bin.

Drama continued into the final two minutes as Gary Prohm struck Ellery Hanley and Lee Crooks called for the ball to take a shot at goal. At 6–4 in their favour the Kiwis were praying that Lee would miss and the odds were in their favour too as the kick was out on the touchline about eight yards inside the New Zealand half, a very long and awkward kick indeed. In came Lee and smack, the ball soared high and straight, right between the posts for what must have been one of the finest goals kicked by all the great kickers in the past. It gave us a draw and squared the series. Jeff had done another great job for his country and again his play belied his almost 37 years. This was also a sad occasion as almost everyone knew that this was indeed Jeff's swan song in international Rugby League. I don't think Great Britain will ever again need to call on a forward of Jeff's age but again I will say that the big man did answer the call with courage, skill and a certain amount of old fashioned panache.

It was in the camp at Shaw Hill for the second Kiwi Test when Peter Fox asked permission to have a private word with

Jeff. I agreed and Jeff and Peter retired to a room where Peter asked Jeff if he would join him at Leeds. Jeff agreed terms of a guaranteed £6,500 per season. The money would be paid in wages and if the £6,500 was not reached during the season then the balance would be paid out as a contractual payment at the season's end. Whilst Jeff and Peter were discussing terms the phone rang and it was Roger Millward, the coach at Hull Kingston Rovers, asking Jeff if he would sign for them. Jeff agreed to join up with Peter at Leeds.

9

FOX, LEEDS AND FEATHERSTONE

Jeff's first game for Leeds was on 3 November 1985 at Wilderspool, Warrington and the side suffered a crushing 32–18 defeat. He was unlucky enough to spring his shoulder on his debut and had two weeks off. Jeff's next game was on 17th November against Hull Kingston Rovers at Headingley. The side lost again 16–12. Barrow beat Leeds in Jeff's third game by 5–2 when the Loiners travelled up to Craven Park, in the first round of the John Player Trophy.

A good result followed when St Helens were held to a 12 points all draw at Knowsley Road but rumblings were heard from disgruntled supporters when Halifax came to Headingley and won 22–20. Cat-calls from the South stand indicated that not all was well with coach Peter Fox's selections and some comments were aimed at Jeff. But all in the garden was rosy within three weeks as Leeds, with Jeff playing as well as ever, produced wins over Castleford away 26–18, Dewsbury at home 28–8, Oldham at home 22–6 and a cracking win at Post Office Road, Featherstone by 20–18.

The Challenge Cup arrived again with a tie against Swinton

at Station Road in the preliminary round. A solid 30–8 win was achieved and Jeff was given a rest until the first round proper of the Challenge Cup when Leeds had drawn Halifax at Thrum Hall, a tough place to go in a cup tie. Leeds won through with a 24–4 win, Jeff recalls:

> Halifax had drawn with Leeds at Thrum Hall before I joined them, then they came to Headingley and won a thrilling game so they were in good spirits when we arrived in the Challenge Cup. It was as tough as ever it was playing Halifax but we had the edge in pace in the backs and it was the three quarters who did the damage scoring all our five tries.

Doncaster were drawn away in round two but requested that the game be played at Headingley to produce a much bigger gate than they would have attracted at Tatters Field. Jeff missed three games because of his back problem and Leeds embarked on one of those unique fixture-league clashes when they had to play Widnes in four consecutive games. The two Widnes league games were played back to back. A loss at Naughton Park for Leeds 20–18, a win at Headingley seven days later 29–12 then seven days later it was back to Naughton Park again to draw magnificently 10 points all with Jeff subbing and coming on to play a vital role in this drama. Three days later it was back to Headingley to witness another tough replay for the right to play Hull Kingston Rovers in the semi final. The score at Leeds in the replay tells all, Leeds 5 Widnes 0. The points came from two David Creaser goals and a Cliff Lyons drop goal giving Jeff another chance to fulfil his cup dream.

The semi final was played at Elland Road and drew a full house. In the most exciting game of football seen for some time the teams could not be separated after 80 minutes and the huge crowd were delighted with the exhibition placed before them. Leeds had a great opportunity to reach Wembley but a Paul Harkins drop goal in the final seconds ensured a second chance for the Robins. The replay was at Elland Road again and another huge crowd saw Hull Kingston Rovers control this game wonderfully with a great 17–nil win. Jeff played in both semi finals but Lady Luck said 'no' and he missed out again.

There also followed a rather disastrous period of league defeats which again antagonised a large band of supporters. Bradford Northern won at Headingley by 28–8, Hull FC won there too by 35–18. Three days later Hull FC won again at The Boulevard 10–4, then Warrington won at Headingley 35–6, a final straw for a lot of Leeds supporters who inundated the board with demands to change the coach and sell a number of the current players. Hull Kingston Rovers beat Leeds at Craven Park 28–12 and Wigan won 29–6 at Central Park. York were beaten 14–12 at Clarence Street and an excellent 38–22 win in the Championship play offs at St Helens sent Leeds to Thrum Hall, Halifax in the play off quarter final only to be beaten 16–13.

There was nothing to show for the cup-hungry Leeds fans. Quite a lot of criticism had been hurled Peter Fox's way in the first and latter part of the season. The club called supporters meetings with the board and the coach but nothing could be smoothed out even after the short term signing of two top Australian centres Mark McGaw and Andrew Ettingshausen.

* * * * *

The 1986–87 season began with a defeat at Oldham and a win against Featherstone Rovers at Headingley but then came a crushing defeat at the hands of St Helens at Leeds and the rumblings began again. Jeff missed the first six games because of his back injury but returned for the big win against Salford at Headingley 46–10. But two heavy defeats prior to the big Salford win had caused problems again between Peter and a section of the crowd as Castleford knocked Leeds out of the Yorkshire Cup at Wheldon Road 38–16 and Widnes ran a 35–10 score past Leeds at Naughton Park. Worse was to come as the Australia touring team recorded a 40–nil victory over Leeds— an unacceptable result. The end of Peter Fox's stay at Leeds came when Warrington travelled to Headingley to inflict a massive defeat on the Loiners 54–16.

The departure of Peter Fox put Jeff in an unusual position. One of the reasons that led to Peter's removal was that the Leeds club were going through a period of bad cash flow. Gates were on a downward trend and season tickets were at an all time low. Consequently there was no money in the kitty to buy their way back to the top. The players brought in by Peter were not considered good enough by the board and there had to be a quick change before matters got any worse. The writer had recently resigned from the post of Great Britain coach and was asked to rejoin the Leeds club in place of Peter.

I accepted, and my first job back at Leeds was to meet with Jeff. He asked if his contract with the club was still ongoing and I replied that that was a matter for Jeff and the board as they had formed this agreement in my absence but I told Jeff I would agree to whatever he wanted. Frank Myler, coaching at Oldham, wanted Jeff with him and the Lancashire club gave Jeff a thorough check up on his back but could not be sure if the injury would go away. Barry Seabourne also wanted Jeff back with him at Odsal. Barry had taken over as coach when Peter had left. Jeff decided to return to Odsal who had received £12,000 from Leeds a short while before to transfer him to Headingley. Barry asked Jeff to see the club specialist about the reoccurrence of the back injury. The specialist gave Jeff a huge injection of cortisone and although it was very painful, this did the job and Jeff was never again troubled by the injury. Jeff returned to Bradford on a much reduced fee.

Jeff played his first match back for Bradford against Featherstone Rovers in the 26–10 win at Post Office Road. Jeff played in the final six games of that season in which Bradford won four and lost two. The games they won were Warrington 11–10, St Helens 18–4 and the one that was most gratifying for Jeff (but not the writer) was Leeds 23–10. Another proud moment for both Jeff and Sue was when son Paul signed professional forms for Bradford in 1986. Jeff and Paul played once at number 8 and 10 in the Bradford Northern 'A' team together and Paul quipped, 'Don't worry dad, I'll look after you!' as they ran onto the field.

But the 1987–88 season was a bitter-sweet one for Jeff. It began well with some great wins against Hull Kingston Rovers in the first round of the County Cup 19–12, another wonderful win over Leeds at Odsal by 32–8, then Bramley 30–6 at McLaren Field in the Yorkshire Cup and Leeds yet again in the Yorkshire Cup semi final at Odsal by 16–5. League wins against Swinton and Halifax put Bradford in a fine mood for the Yorkshire Cup final at Headingley against Castleford.

Bradford Northern Versus Castleford, Yorkshire Cup Final, Headingley, Leeds, 17 October 1987

It was good for Jeff to walk out at Leeds with the Bradford team as it gave him another chance to show the Leeds club it had been a mistake to let him go. It was a tough final where not a lot of open football was played but it was an intriguing game as first one team looked to get on top then the other came back at them. Scorers for Castleford were Plange and Linder tries with Ketteridge kicking two goals and for Northern Fairbank one try and Mumby and Hobbs two goals each in a tough 12 all draw. The replay was at Elland Road 14 days later but first Bradford had to play Hull Kingston Rovers at Odsal in the league. The bitter blow for Jeff was that in attempting one of his trade mark drive, turn and pass to supporting players, he turned in the tackle and suddenly heard and felt two loud cracks! He had broken both his tibia and fibula bones in his leg. The injury would have been bad enough for a younger player but at Jeff's age it looked like the end of a great career. He was now approaching 39 years old and surely he couldn't come back after this serious injury. But this was Jeff Grayshon who never took a backward step.

*　*　*　*　*

Nine months later Jeff kicked off the 1988–89 season with his old mate Peter Fox at Featherstone Rovers having been allowed a free transfer. The dedication of the man can be seen in that he played in every match except one in his first season at Post Office Road. The team had some tremendous results that first season with notable wins including the 'double' over St Helens in the league by 13–12 at Saints and 31–10 at Featherstone. The team scored a 'double' also against the strong Hull Kingston Rovers 30–15 away and 28–6 at home was recorded with a magnificent win at Odsal against his old club Bradford by 32–23. Out of the 25 games played by Jeff in the league, 14 were won and one drawn. Of the nine cup ties Jeff played in, five were won and there was another proud moment when Featherstone went to Headingley in the Championship play offs and beat Leeds 15–12.

In the season 1989–90 Jeff again missed starting in only one game for the club, although he subbed in that game. It was against the touring Kiwis. Two days before the Kiwi game Featherstone had gallantly fought their way to the Yorkshire Cup final after beating Keighley in round one, Doncaster in the second round and drawing at home to Castleford in round three 18 points all. Featherstone won the replay 28–26 and the other team in the final was Bradford Northern!

Featherstone Rovers Versus Bradford Northern, Yorkshire Cup Final, Headingley, Leeds, 5 November 1989

Gerald Cordle and Paul Harkin scored two tries each and David Hobbs kicked two goals for Bradford and Ivor Ropati and Peter Smith scored tries and Deryck Fox kicked three goals for Featherstone. Bradford lifted the Yorkshire Cup with a score of 20–14 but it was a close run thing.

The season 1990–91 was another good one for Jeff. When Peter Fox had signed Jeff for Featherstone he offered him a contract for three years for £21,000. This was the final year of the contract. Of the 33 cup and league games played by the Rovers, Jeff figured in 32, only twice as a substitute. It was early season when Featherstone Rovers played Bradford at Post Office Road and it was a close game with Bradford winning 26–24. One of Rugby League's folklore tales comes from this game. Jeff was playing for the first time against his son Paul. Although Paul was packing at blind side prop he had no contact with his dad who was at open side prop.

Bradford kicked off after a Featherstone try and Jeff was stationed on the touchline about 20 yards inside his own half. The kick went high and Jeff took the ball just as Paul arrived. He caught his dad in the ribcage and knocked Jeff arse over tit onto the muddy ground where he slid on his backside until he was stopped by thudding into the advertising boards around the ground. Jeff sat there, the wind taken out of his sails, and stood directly above Jeff was this experienced mature former miner puffing on his Woodbine. Looking down on Jeff he said without a flicker of emotion, 'If I were thee Jeff, I'd smack his arse and send him to bed!' It brought the house down for those hearing these words of wisdom. Whether this tale is true or not, I couldn't say but it epitomises the humour that was in the game then. I would like to think it was true.

The most notable win of this season was in the Championship play offs when Featherstone went to Central Park and beat Wigan 31–26. Jeff had played as well as ever in this season so it was a shock when the secretary wrote to Jeff and explained that the club would not require his services next season. They thanked him for all his great work for the club. Peter Fox was on holiday when the letter arrived and when he returned home he was furious that the board would do such a thing to someone who had given so much to the game. Peter said that he wanted Jeff for next season but the board would not give way so Peter resigned as Featherstone coach on principle. He came across to see Jeff and Sue and made it right that he had nothing to do with the business.

10

MOUNT PLEASANT AND THE PALACE

Jeff was contacted by his old mate David Ward, then the Batley coach, who asked him if he would come to Mount Pleasant and do a job for him with his young team in division two of the Rugby Football League. Jeff remembers, 'What else could I do? I was still fit enough to play and playing with young and enthusiastic players would make my job that bit easier. So I said yes to Wardy and went up to the Mount'. Wayne Heron and Steve Parrish had joined Batley from Bradford so Jeff knew several of the players when he went training on the first night. Jeff played in 29 of the 33 games Batley played in that season and subbed once, making 30 of the 33 played. The club only lost seven league games and in the division two Play offs beat Barrow at home and Leigh away falling to Sheffield Eagles away at the final hurdle.

In September 1992 Jeff received an official looking letter. Inside the envelope was a notification from Buckingham Palace that he had been nominated for the award of the MBE for services to Rugby League Football. It said that he would be advised if the nomination had been accepted by Her Royal Majesty the Queen and told to keep it a secret until the Palace announced it to the press. Jeff's wife Sue takes up the story:

> We were informed that Jeff had been accepted and the award would be presented at the Palace on 28th October on our 25th wedding anniversary. We travelled down by train and booked in at the St James Palace Hotel. The occasion was unbelievable, quite marvellous. We entered the Palace and were ushered into a huge room and there Jeff was taken, with all the other recipients, to another room where they were advised what to do and say and how to address Her Majesty should she speak to them. We were ushered to the viewing area and I was given a beautiful seat right at the front. There were at least two or three hundred people in this big room and they were whispering and talking in low voices when suddenly Her Majesty walked slowly into the room with her two Corgi dogs. The room fell into utter silence and Her Majesty walked to the shallow dais and the first name was gently called out to come forward to receive an award.
>
> Soon the official called, 'Mr Jeffrey Grayshon,' and out stepped Jeff, looking immaculate in his morning suit.
>
> The Queen said a few words, 'You have been awarded the MBE for services to your sport which I am told is a Northern Sport called Rugby League. Well done and the best of luck to you'.
>
> Her Majesty pinned on the award and Jeff gently bowed and walked slowly backwards so as not to turn his back on the Queen until he had reached a marker on the floor. So my husband was now Jeff Grayshon MBE and I was immensely proud of him. We were advised that we could have photographs taken but as the ceremony ended there was a rush to get in first for the photos. This was not at all what one would expect in the Palace. We spent the night in London then travelled back a day later when we had arranged a party for family and friends at David Wards hotel in Birstall and we had a great night.

The great Jeff Grayshon's final season was in 1994–95 when Jeff had taken the player-coach roll. He subbed in all 17 games the club had in the second division and was the grand old age of 45.

I asked Jeff if he had any regrets in the 25 years he had played and true to the man he is answered:

> None whatsoever. I would not have swapped it for anything. I met and played with, and against, some great blokes. I made some great friendships, I played under some excellent coaches and had Chairmen who, in the most part, treated me right, especially Steve Ball as chairman at Batley who nominated me for the MBE. I mostly have to thank Sue who kept me going when all seemed lost and Paul and the grandkids as well. Regrets? Not on your life. Anybody want an experienced prop?

Jeff and Sue's grandchildren, Mark and Natalie are now 21 and 20 respectively. Natalie works in a bank and Mark actually continued the Grayshon tradition by playing Rugby League for Salford. But a few years ago, Jeff went into hospital for a knee replacement and whilst on the operating table suffered two strokes leaving him paralysed down his right side. He lost his speech but that returned fairly quickly. Now he is back to virtual normality. The doctors at Dewsbury Hospital believe that Jeff's long term playing career helped him back to health as he could focus on getting well thanks to his competitive spirit through all the years of training and playing. Also he was renowned for injuries repairing quickly and that could have something to do with his resolute spirit and determination. He again goes down to tend to his livestock at his allotment in Birstall, he keeps chickens and turkeys but Jeff says the turkeys become very nervous at Christmas time.

Jeff's playing career was amazingly long—few players are able to continue playing Rugby League well into their forties. His resilience and strength were awesome and he thoroughly earned his MBE. Jeff deserves his name to be long remembered as he was truly The Warrior of Rugby League.

Appendix

Team Lists of Highlighted Games in Main Text

CHAPTER 1

Dewsbury Versus Oldham, Watersheddings, 26 September 1970 (first team debut, listing for Dewsbury only)

Rushton; Childe, Grayshon, Nigel Stephenson, Yoward; Agar, Alan Bates; Naylor, Mick Stephenson, Taylor, Rhodes, John Bates and Robinson, subs Hayman and Joe Boocock.

CHAPTER 2

Dewsbury Versus Leeds, Odsal Stadium, Yorkshire Cup Final, 7 October 1972

Dewsbury team: Adrian Rushton; Greg Ashcroft, Alan Childe, Terry Day, Geoff Yoward; Alan Agar, Alan Bates; Graham Bell, Mick Stephenson, Dick Lowe, Jeff Grayshon, John Bates and Steve Hankins, the subs were Steve Lee and Harry Beverley. *Leeds team*: John Holmes; Alan Smith, Syd Hynes, Les Dyl, John Atkinson; Alan Hardisty, Keith Hepworth; Terry Clawson, David Ward, Bill Ramsey, Phil Cookson, Graham Eccles and Ray Batten and their subs were John Langley and Tony Fisher.

Dewsbury Versus Leeds, Championship Final, Odsal Stadium, 19 May 1973

Dewsbury team: Adrian Rushton; Greg Ashcroft, John Clark, Nigel Stephenson, Terry Day; Alan Agar, Alan Bates; Harry Beverley, Mick Stephenson, Dick Lowe, Jeff Grayshon, John Bates and Joe Whittington with Steve Lee and Brian Taylor as subs. *Leeds team*: John Holmes; Alan Smith, Syd Hynes, Les Dyl, John Atkinson; Alan Hardisty, Keith Hepworth;Terry Clawson, Tony Fisher, Geoff Clarkson, Phil Cookson, Graham Eccles and Bob Haigh.

Yorkshire Versus Lancashire, Naughton Park, Widnes, 19 September 1973

Lancashire team: Derek Whitehead [Warrington]; Norman Brelsford [Rochdale Hornets], Billy Benyon [St Helens], Chris Hesketh [Salford], Eric Hughes [Widnes]; David Eckersley [St Helens], Parry Gordon [Warrington]; Jim Fiddler [Leigh], Dick Evans [Swinton], Brian Brady [Warrington], George Nicholls [St Helens], Bob Welding [Rochdale Hornets] and Eric Prescott [Salford], the subs were, Derek Noonan [Warrington] and Barry Briggs [Warrington]. *Yorkshire team*: Brian Jefferson [Keighley]; Alan Smith [Leeds]. Syd Hynes [Leeds], John Holmes [Leeds], John Atkinson [Leeds]; David Topliss [Wakefield Trinity], Steve Nash [Featherstone Rovers]; Mick Harrison [Hull FC], Mick Morgan [Wakefield Trinity], Frank Davies [Huddersfield], Jimmy Thompson [Featherstone Rovers], Jeff Grayshon [Dewsbury] and Charlie Stone [Featherstone Rovers]. Subs: John Bates [Dewsbury] and Geoff Wraith [Wakefield Trinity]. Referee: Mr Billy Thompson of Huddersfield, attendance 3,357.

CHAPTER 3

Yorkshire Versus Cumbria, Derwent Park, Workington, 11 September 1974

Yorkshire team: Brian Jefferson [Keighley]; Mike Lamb [Bradford Northern], David Hartley [Featherstone Rovers], Mike Smith [Featherstone Rovers], David Redfearn [Bradford Northern]; David Topliss [Wakefield Trinity], Steve Nash [Featherstone Rovers]; Mick Harrison [Leeds], Bob Spurr [Castleford], Vince Farrar [Featherstone Rovers], Jeff Grayshon [Dewsbury], John Bates [Dewsbury] and Steve Norton [Castleford]. Subs: Bruce Burton [Halifax] and Bill Ramsey [Bradford Northern]. *Cumbria team*: Paul Charlton [Salford]; John Risman [Workington Town], Bob Nicholson [Workington Town], Ian Wright [Workington Town], Ken Gallagher [Whitehaven]; Graham Mather [Whitehaven], Arnie Walker [Workington Town], Steve Hogan [Barrow], Allan Banks [Workington Town], Ralph Calvin [Workington Town], Les Gorley [Workington Town], Dave Curwen [Workington Town] and Gordon Cottier [Whitehaven]. Subs: John Cunningham [Barrow] and Harry Marland [Workington Town]. Referee: Mr Alec Givvons of Oldham, attendance 788.

Yorkshire Versus Other Nationalities, Craven Park, Hull, 18 September 1974

Yorkshire team: David Marshall [Leeds]; David Redfearn [Bradford Northern], John Hughes [Bramley], Mike Smith [Featherstone Rovers], John Atkinson [Leeds]; Bruce Burton [Halifax], Alan Bates [Dewsbury]; Mick Harrison [Leeds], Vince Farrar [Featherstone Rovers], Bill Ramsey [Bradford Northern], Jeff Grayshon [Dewsbury], Jimmy Thompson [Featherstone Rovers] and Steve Norton [Castleford]. Subs: John Langley [Leeds] and John Bates [Dewsbury]. *Other Nationalities team*: Dickie Wallace [York]; Robert Fleay [Swinton], David Willicombe [Wigan], Green Vigo [Wigan], David Barends [York]; Ray Wilkins [Blackpool Borough], Bak Diabiora [Bradford Northern]; Jim Mills [Widnes], Tony Fisher [Leeds], Brian Butler [Swinton], Stewart Gallacher [Bradford Northern], Frannie Jarvis [Bradford Northern] and Colin Dixon [Salford]. Subs: Bob Smithies [Hull Kingston Rovers] and Peter Rowe [Blackpool Borough]. Referee: Mr Mick Naughton of Widnes, attendance 727.

Yorkshire Versus Lancashire, Lawkholme Lane, Keighley, 25 September 1974

Yorkshire team: David Marshall [Leeds]; David Redfearn [Bradford Northern], Peter Roe, John Hughes [Bramley], John Atkinson [Leeds]: Roger Millward [Hull Kingston Rovers]. Alan Bates [Dewsbury]; Mal Dixon [York], Dean Raistrick, Bob Irving [Wigan], Jeff Grayshon [Dewsbury], Graham Idle [Bramley] and Steve Norton [Castleford]. Subs: Garry Clark [New Hunslet] and John Bates [Dewsbury]. *Lancashire team*: Derek Whitehead [Warrington]; Stuart Wright [Wigan], John Walsh [St Helens], Chris Hesketh [Salford], Eric Hughes [Widnes]; Alan Whittle [Warrington], Parry Gordon [Warrington]; Dave Chisnall [Warrington], Dick Evans [Swinton], Jimmy Fiddler [Leigh], Tommy Martyn [Leigh], Brian Gregory [Oldham] and Barry Philbin [Warrington]. Subs: Dave Robinson [Wigan] and Jimmy Nulty [Wigan]. Referee: Mr Harry Hunt of Prestbury, attendance 1,219.

Lancashire Versus Yorkshire, County Championship Final, Naughton Park, Widnes, 16 October 1974

Lancashire team: Ray Dutton [Widnes]; Stuart Wright [Wigan], Chris Hesketh [Salford], Derek Noonan [Warrington], Eric Hughes [Widnes]; Ken Gill [Salford], Parry Gordon [Warrington]; Dave Chisnall [Warrington], Kevin Ashcroft [Warrington], Brian Brady [Warrington], George Nicholls [St Helens], Eric Prescott [Salford] and Barry Philbin [Warrington]. Subs: Mal Aspey [Widnes] and Tommy Martyn [Leigh]. *Yorkshire team*: Les Sheard [Wakefield Trinity]; Mike Lamb [Bradford Northern], Peter Roe [Keighley], Bruce Burton [Halifax], John Atkinson [Leeds]; David Topliss [Wakefield Trinity], Alan Bates [Dewsbury]; Mal Dixon [York], Dean Raistrick [Keighley], John Millington [Hull Kingston Rovers], Jeff Grayshon [Dewsbury], Bob Irving [Wigan] and Steve Norton [Castleford], the subs were John Hughes [Bramley] and Mick Morgan [Wakefield Trinity]. Referee: Mr Joe Jackson of Pudsey, attendance 3,114.

England Versus Wales, World Championship, Wilderspool Stadium, Warrington, 20 September 1975

England team: George Fairbairn [Wigan]; Keith Fielding [Salford], Eric Hughes [Widnes], John Holmes [Leeds], John Atkinson [Leeds]; Kenny Gill [Salford], Roger Millward [Hull Kingston Rovers, captain]; Brian Hogan [Wigan], Keith Bridges [Featherstone Rovers], Colin Forsyth [Bradford Northern], Bob Irving [Wigan], Jeff Grayshon [Dewsbury] and Steve Norton [Castleford]. Subs: Dave Eckersley [St Helens] and George Nicholls [St Helens]. *Wales team*: Bill Francis [Wigan]; Clive Sullivan [Hull Kingston Rovers], Dai Watkins [Salford], Frank Wilson [St Helens], John Bevan [Warrington]; David Treasure [Oldham], Peter Banner [Salford]; John Mantle [St Helens], Tony Fisher [Castleford], Mel James [St Helens], Brian Gregory [Wigan], Eddie Cunningham [St Helens] and Kel Coslett [St Helens. Subs: Glen Turner [Hull Kingston Rovers] and Peter Rowe [Blackpool Borough]. Referee was M. Caillol of France, attendance 5,034.

England Versus France, Bordeaux, 11 October 1975

England team: George Fairbairn [Wigan]; Keith Fielding [Salford], Eric Hughes [Widnes], John Holmes [Leeds], John Atkinson [Leeds]; Kenny Gill [Salford], Roger Millward [Hull Kingston Rovers, captain]; Brian Hogan [Wigan], Keith Bridges [Featherstone Rovers], Colin Forsyth [Bradford Northern], Bob Irving [Wigan], Jeff Grayshon [Dewsbury] and Steve Norton [Castleford]. Subs: Dave Eckersley [St Helens] and George Nicholls [St Helens]. *French team*: M. De Matos [Toulouse]; J.F. Grechi [Limoux], Andre Ruiz [Pau], R. Terrats [St Esteve], M. Laffargue [Tonneins]; Jose Calle [St Esteve captain], J.M. Imbert [Avignon]; G. Garcia [Carcassonne], F. Duthil [Bordeaux], A. Gonzales [Villeneuve], J.M. Bosc [St Esteve], J.P. Tremouille [Tonneins] and G. Buchi [Marseilles]. Subs: C. Thenegal [Toulouse] and G.V. Vigouroux [Tonneins].

England Versus New Zealand, Odsal Stadium, Bradford, 26 October 1975

England team: George Fairbairn [Wigan]; Stuart Wright [Wigan], Eric Hughes [Widnes], John Holmes [Leeds], Ged Dunn [Hull Kingston Rovers]; Kenny Gill [Salford], Roger Millward [Hull Kingston Rovers captain]; Brian Hogan [Wigan],

Keith Bridges [Featherstone Rovers], Colin Forsyth [Bradford Northern], Jeff Grayshon [Dewsbury], Mick Adams [Widnes] and Steve Norton [Castleford]. Subs: Les Dyl [Leeds] and George Nicholls [St Helens]. *New Zealand team*: Warren Callicoat [Auckland]; Phil Orchard [Wellington], James Smith [Auckland], Dennis Williams [Auckland], Bruce Dickenson [Canterbury]; Bob Jarvis [Auckland], Ken Stirling [Auckland]; Lynn Proctor [Auckland], Tom Conroy [Auckland], John Greengrass [Canterbury], Bob Baxendale [West Coast], Tony Coll [West Coast] and Mark Eade [Auckland]. Subs: Alan Gordon [Auckland] and Paul Gurnick [Auckland].

England Versus Australia, Central Park, Wigan, 1 November 1975

Australian team: Graham Eadie [Manley]; Ian Shubert [Eastern Suburbs], Johnny Brass [Eastern Suburbs], Mick Cronin [Gerringong], Johnny Rhodes [Wynnum Manley]; Johnny Peard [Eastern Suburbs], Johnny Mayes [Eastern Suburbs]; Arthur Beetson [Eastern Suburbs, captain], George Piggins [South Sydney], Ian Mackay [Eastern Suburbs], Ray Higgs [Parramatta], Terry Randall [Manley] and Greg Pierce [Cronulla]. Sub: Steve Rogers [Conulla]. England team: George Fairbairn [Wigan]; Ged Dunn [Hull Kingston Rovers], John Holmes [Leeds]. Les Dyl [Leeds], David Redfearn [Bradford Northern]; Kenny Gill [Salford], Roger Millward [Hull Kingston Rovers, captain]; Brian Hogan [Wigan], Keith Bridges [Featherstone Rovers], Jimmy Thompson [Featherstone Rovers], Jeff Grayshon [Dewsbury], Bob Irving [Wigan] and Steve Norton [Castleford]. Subs: Eric Hughes [Widnes] and Mick Adams [Widnes].

England Versus Australia, Headingley, Leeds, 12 November 1975

Australian team: Graham Eadie [Manly]; Ian Schubert [Eastern Suburbs], Steve Rogers [Cronulla], Mick Cronin [Gerringong], Johnny Rhodes [Wynnum Manley]; Johnny Peard [Eastern Suburbs], Tom Raudonikis [Western Suburbs]; Arthur Beetson [Eastern Suburbs], Johnny Lang [Eastern Suburbs], Greg Vievers [South Brisbane], Ray Higgs [Parramatta], Terry Randall [Manly] and Greg Pierce [Cronulla]. Subs: Jim Porter [Eastern Suburbs] and Ian MacKay [Eastern Suburbs]. *England team*: Ray Dutton [Widnes]; David Smith [Wakefield Trinity], Eric Hughes [Widnes], Nigel Stephenson [Dewsbury], Ged Dunn [Hull Kingston Rovers]; Ken Gill [Salford], Roger Millward [Hull Kingston Rovers]; Harry Beverley [Dewsbury], Keith Bridges [Featherstone Rovers], Jimmy Thompson [Featherstone Rovers], Jeff Grayshon [Dewsbury], Mick Adams [Widnes] and Stan Fearnley [Bradford Northern]: Subs: David Topliss [Wakefield Trinity] and Charlie Stone [Featherstone Rovers].Referee: Mr Fred Lindop of Wakefield, attendance 7,727.

Dewsbury Versus St Helens, BBC2 Floodlit Trophy Final, Knowsley Road, 16 December 1975

Saints team: Geoff Pimblett; Les Jones, Billy Benyon, Dave Hull, Roy Mathias; Frank Wilson, Jeff Heaton; John Mantle. Tony Karalius, Mel James, George Niclolls, Eric Chisnall and Kel Coslett. *Dewsbury team*: John Langley; John Hegarty, Greg Chalkley, Ian Simpson, Gary Mitchell; Nigel Stephenson, Alan Bates; Harry Beverley, Ray Price, Steve Hankins, Steve Halloran, Graham Bell and Jeff Grayshon, the subs were Steve Lee and Phil Artis.

Cumbria Versus Yorkshire, Crown Flatt, Dewsbury 19 November 1975

Yorkshire team: Geoff Wraith [Castleford]; David Smith [Wakefield Trinity], John Holmes [Leeds], Les Dyl [Leeds], Ged Dunn [Hull Kingston Rovers]; John Newlove [Featherstone Rovers], Roger Millward [Hull Kingston Rovers]; Harry Beverley [Dewsbury], Keith Bridges [Featherstone Rovers], Jimmy Thompson [Featherstone Rovers], Jeff Grayshon [Dewsbury]; Bob Irving [Wigan] and Steve Norton [Castleford]. Subs: Nigel Stephenson [Dewsbury] and Mick Morgan [Wakefield Trinity]. *Cumbria team*: Harry Marsland [Workington Town]; John Risman [Workington Town], Paul Charlton [Workington Town], Phil Clegg [Barrow]; Bob Nicholson [Workington Town], Arnie Walker [Workington Town]; Steve Hogan [Barrow], Allan Banks [Workington Town], John 'Spanky' McFarlane [Whitehaven], Les Gorley [Workington Town], Harold Henney [Workington Town] and Bob Blackwood [Wigan]. Subs: Denis Jackson [Barrow] and Eddie Bowman [Workington Town]. Referee: Mr Vinnie Moss of Manchester, attendance 1,500.

Yorkshire Versus Other Nationalities, Odsal Stadium, Bradford, 6 December 1975

Yorkshire team: Geoff Wraith [Castleford]; David Smith [Wakefield Trinity], John Holmes [Leeds], Nigel Stephenson [Dewsbury], Ged Dunn [Hull Kingston Rovers]; John Newlove [Featherstone Rovers], Steve Nash [Salford]; Harry Beverley [Dewsbury], Keith Bridges [Featherstone Rovers], Jimmy Thompson [Featherstone Rovers], Jeff Grayshon [Dewsbury]; Bob Irving [Wigan] and Steve Norton [Castleford]. Subs: David Topliss [Wakefield Trinity] and Mick Morgan [Wakefield Trinity]. Other Nationalities team: Dickie Wallace [Hull Kingston Rovers]; David Barends [York], Harold Box [Featherstone Rovers], Green Vigo [Wigan], Rudy Francis [Bradford Northern]: Frank Wilson [St Helens], Steve Martin [Barrow]; Bruce Gibbs [Workington Town], Don Parry [Huyton], Chris Forster [Bramley], Peter Rowe [Blackpool Borough], Paul Souter [New Hunslet] and John Knighton [Salford]. Subs: Chris Hill [Featherstone Rovers] and Ron Pomering [Bramley]. Referee: Mr Stan Wall of Leigh, attendance 737.

Lancashire versus Yorkshire, Central Park, Wigan, 20 December 1975

Yorkshire team: John Langley [Dewsbury]; David Smith [Wakefield Trinity], John Holmes [Leeds], Les Dyl [Leeds], John Atkinson [Leeds]; David Topliss [Wakefield Trinity], Gary Stephens [Castleford]; John Millington [Hull Kingston Rovers], Keith Bridges [Featherstone Rovers], Vince Farrar [Featherstone Rovers], Jeff Grayshon [Dewsbury], Mick Morgan [Wakefield Trinity] and Steve Norton [Castleford]. Subs: Brian Hancock [Hull FC] and Jimmy Thompson [Featherstone Rovers]. *Lancashire team*: Ray Dutton [Widnes]; Les Jones [St Helens], John Butler [Salford], Mick George [Widnes], Eric Hughes [Widnes]; Ken Gill [Salford], Reg Bowden [Widnes], Brian Hogan [Wigan], Dickie Evans [Swinton], Alan Hodkinson [Rochdale Hornets], Sammy Turnbull [Salford], Tommy Martyn [Warrington] and Mick Adams [Widnes]. Subs: Billy Benyon [St Helens] and Nick Nelson [Widnes]. Referee: Mr Kevin Allatt of Huddersfield, attendance 700.

CHAPTER 4

England Versus Wales, European Championship, Headingley, Leeds, 29 January 1977

England team: George Fairbairn [Wigan]; Stuart Wright [Widnes], John Holmes [Leeds], Les Dyl [Leeds], Les Jones [St Helens]; Kenny Gill [Salford], Roger Millward [Hull Kingston Rovers, captain]; Brian Hogan [Wigan], Keith Bridges [Featherstone Rovers], Jimmy Thompson [Featherstone Rovers], Jeff Grayshon [Dewsbury], Les Gorley [Workington Town] and Doug Laughton [Widnes]. Subs: David Eckersley [Widnes] and Malcolm Reilly [Castleford]. *Welsh team*: Dai Watkins [Salford, captain]; Roy Mathias [St Helens], John Bevan [Warrington], Eddie Cunningham [St Helens], Maurice Richards [Salford]; Bill Francis [Wigan], Paul Woods [Widnes]; Jim Mills [Workington Town], Tony Fisher [Castleford], John Mantle [Salford], Mike Nicholas [Warrington], Colin Dixon [Salford] and Peter Rowe [Huddersfield]. Subs: Rob Wilkins [Workington Town] and Mick Murphy [Bradford Northern]. Referee: Mr Billy Thompson of Huddersfield, attendance 6,472.

Yorkshire Versus Cumbria, Recreation Ground, Whitehaven, 15 February 1977

Cumbrian team: Paul Charlton [Workington Town]; Ian MacCorquodale [Workington Town], John Risman [Workington Town], Rob Wilkins [Workington Town], Phil Clegg [Barrow]; Ray McConnell [Barrow], Arnie Walker [Workington Town]; Jim Hamilton [Blackpool Borough], Howard Allen [Barrow], Eddie Bowman [Workington Town], Les Gorley [Workington Town], Martin Flynn [Barrow] and Tom Gainford [Whitehaven]. Subs: Ian Holland [Barrow] and Gordon Cottier [Whitehaven]. *Yorkshire team*: Geoff Wraith [Castleford]; Peter Muscroft [New Hunslet], John Joiner [Castleford], Peter Roe [Bradford Northern], John Atkinson [Leeds]; David Topliss [Wakefield Trinity], Gary Stephens [Castleford]; Jimmy Thompson [Featherstone Rovers], David Ward [Leeds], Allan Dickinson [Castleford], Jeff Grayshon [Dewsbury], Sammy Lloyd [Castleford], Mick Morgan [Wakefield Trinity]. Subs: Mike Smith [Hull Kingston Rovers] and Vince Farrar [Featherstone Rovers]. Referee: Mr Vinnie Moss of Manchester, attendance 3,000.

CHAPTER 5

England Versus Wales, European Championship, Naughton Park, Widnes, 16 March 1979

England team: Keith Mumby [Bradford Northern]; Stewart Wright [Widnes], Peter Glynn [St Helens], Keith Smith [Wakefield Trinity],Eric Hughes [Widnes]; Ken Kelly [Warrington], Gary Stephens [Castleford]; Harry Beverley [Workington Town], Graham Liptrot [St. Helens], Brian Lockwood [Hull Kingston Rovers, captain], Tommy Martyn [Warrington], Jeff Grayshon [Bradford Northern] and Mick Adams [Widnes]. Subs: John Woods [Leigh] and David Watkinson [Hull Kingston Rovers]. *Welsh team*: Harold Box [Featherstone Rovers]; Clive Sullivan [Hull Kingston Rovers], John Risman [Workington Town], John Bevan [Warrington], Brian Juliff [Wakefield Trinity]; Bill Francis [St Helens], Paul Woods [Rochdale Hornets]; Jim

Mills [Widnes], Tommy Cunningham [Warrington], Mel James [St Helens], Trevor Skerrett [Wakefield Trinity], Peter Rowe [Huddersfield] and Roy Mathias [St Helens]. Subs: Paul Prenderville [Hull FC] and Mike Nicholas [St Helens]. Referee: Mr Ronnie Campbell of Widnes, attendance 5,099.

England Versus France, European Championship, Wilderspool, Warrington, 24 March 1979

England team: Keith Mumby [Bradford Northern]; Stuart Wright [Widnes]. Peter Glynn [St Helens], John Woods [Leigh], Eric Hughes [Widnes]; Steve Evans [Featherstone Rovers], Alan Redfearn [Bradford Northern]; Keith Tindall [Hull FC], Graham Liptrot [St Helens], Brian Lockwood [Hull Kingston Rovers, captain], Jeff Grayshon [Bradford Northern], Tommy Martyn [Warrington] and Phil Hogan [Hull Kingston Rovers]. Subs: Barry Banks [York] and Eddie Szymala [Barrow]. French team: A-- Touchagues [Catalan]; Jon-Paul Sire [Catalan], Claud Laumond [Villefranche], M-- Noudo [Catalan], J-- Moya [Carcassonne]; Eric Walligunda [Lezignan], Guy Alard [Carcassonne]; Henri Daniel [Pia], A-- Malacamp [Carcassonne], Delphin Castanon [Lezignan], C-- Zaluendo [Toulouse], D-- Hermet [Villeneuve] and M-- Maique [Lezignan]. Subs: M--Fidou [ ] and R-- Terrats [St Esteve]. Referee: Mon. A. Breysse of Marseilles, attendance 5,004.

Bradford Northern Versus Leeds, Premiership Final, Fartown, Huddersfield, 27 May 1979

Bradford Northern team: Keith Mumby: Derek Parker, Eddie Oculicz, Les Gant, Alan Spencer; Steve Ferres, Alan Redfearn; Jimmy Thompson, Keith Bridges, Colin Forsyth, Dennis Trotter, Jeff Grayshon and Len Casey. Subs: George Mordue and Ian Van Bellen. *Leeds team*: Neil Hague; Alan Smith, David Smith, Les Dyl, John Atkinson; Kevin Dick, Sammy Sanderson; Mick Harrison, David Ward, Steve Pitchford, Mick Joyce, Graham Eccles and Phil Cookson. Subs: Paul Fletcher and Butch Adams.

CHAPTER 6

Lions Versus Australia, First Test, Lang Park, Brisbane, 16 June 1979

Australian team: Graham Eadie [Manly]; Kerry Boustead [Eastern Suburbs], Steve Rogers [Cronulla], Mick Cronin [Parramatta], Larry Corowa [Balmain]; Alan Thompson [Manly], Tommy Raudonikis [Western Suburbs]; Craig Young [St George], George Peponis [Canterbury-Bankstown captain], Rod Morris [Balmain], Les Boyd [Western Suburbs], Rod Reddy [St George] and Ray Price [Parramatta]. Subs: Alan McMahon [Balmain] and Ray Brown [Western Suburbs]. *Great Britain*: John Woods [Leigh]; David Barens [Bradford Northern], John Joyner [Castleford], Eric Hughes [Widnes], Roy Mathias [St Helens]; John Holmes [Leeds], Gary Stephens [Castleford]; Jim Mills [Widnes], David Ward [Leeds], Trevor Skerrett [Wakefield Trinity], Doug Laughton [Widnes captain], George Nicholls and Steve Norton [Hull FC]. Subs: Steve Evans [Featherstone Rovers] and Phil Hogan [Hull Kingston Rovers]. Referee: Mr E. Ward of Queensland, attendance 23,051.

Lions Versus Australia, Second Test, Sydney Cricket Ground, 30 June 1979

Australian team: Graham Eadie [Manly]; Kerry Boustead [Eastern Suburbs], Steve Rogers [Cronulla], Mick Cronin [Parramatta], Larry Corowa [Balmain]; Alan Thompson [Manly], Tommy Raudonikis [Western Suburbs]; Craig Young [St George], George Peponis [Canterbury-Bankstown captain], Rod Morris [Balmain], Les Boyd [Western Suburbs], Rod Reddy [St George] and Ray Price [Parramatta]. Subs: Alan McMahon [Balmain] and Ray Brown [Western Suburbs]. *Great Britain*: George Fairbairn [Wigan]; David Barends [Bradford Northern], John Joyner [Castleford], John Woods [Leigh], Eric Hughes [Widnes]; John Holmes [Leeds], Gary Stephens [Castleford]; George Nicholls, [St Helens, captain], David Ward [Leeds], Trevor Skerrett [Wakefield Trinity], Len Casey [Bradford Northern], Jeff Grayshon [Bradford Northern] and Mick Adams [Widnes]. Subs: Steve Evans [Featherstone Rovers] and David Watkinson [Hull Kingston Rovers]. The Referee was Mr Greg Hartley of New South Wales and the attendance was 26,387.

Lions Versus Australia, Third Test, Sydney Cricket Ground, 14 July 1979

Australian Team: Graham Eadie [Manly]; Chris Anderson [Canterbury-Bankstown], Steve Rogers [Cronulla], Mick Cronin [Parramatta], Terry Fahey [South Sydney]; Alan Thompson [Manly] Tommy Raudonikis [Western Suburbs]; Craig Young [St, George], George Peponis [Canterbury-Bankstown, captain], Rod Morris [Balmain], Les Boyd [Western Suburbs], Rod Reddy [St. George] and Ray Price [Parramatta], the subs were Allan McMahon [Balmain] and Ray Brown [Western Suburbs]. *Great Britain*: George Fairbairn [Wigan]; Steve Evans [Featherstone Rovers], John Joyner [Castleford], John Woods [Leigh], Eric Hughes [Widnes]; David Topliss [Wakefield Trinity], Alan Redfearn [Bradford Northern]; George Nicholls [St, Helens, captain], David Ward [Leeds], Len Casey [Bradford Northern], Phil Hogan [Hull Kingston Rovers], Jeff Grayshon [Bradford Northern], and Steve Norton [Hull FC], the Lions subs were John Holmes [Leeds] and Mick Adams [Widnes]. The Referee was Mr. E. Ward of Queensland and the attendance was 16,854.

Lions Versus New Zealand, First Test, Carlaw Park, Auckland, 21 July 1979

New Zealand: Warren Collicoat [Wellington]; Dick Uluave [Manawatu], James Leuluai [Auckland], Olsen Filipaina [Auckland], Dane O'Hara [Auckland]: Fred Ah Kuoi [Auckland], Gordon Smith [West Coast]; Mark Broadhurst [Canterbury], Howie Tamati [Taranaki], Dane Sorenson [Cronulla, Australia], Graham West [Taranaki, captain], Kevin Tamati [Wellington] and Tony Coll [West Coast]. Subs: David Smith [Auckland] and Paul Ravlich [Waikato]. Lions: George Fairbairn [Wigan]; Steve Evans [Featherstone Rovers], John Joyner [Castleford], Mike Smith [Hull Kingston Rovers], Eric Hughes [Widnes]; John Holmes [Leeds], Gary Stephens [Castleford]; George Nicholls [St Helens, captain], David Ward [Leeds], Len Casey [Bradford Northern], Phil Hogan [Hull Kingston Rovers], Jeff Grayshon [Bradford Northern] and Mick Adams [Widnes]. Subs: Peter Glynn [St Helens] and Brian Lockwood [Hull Kingston Rovers]. Referee: Mr John Percival of Auckland, attendance 9,200.

Lions Versus New Zealand, Second Test, Addington Show Ground, Christchurch, 5 August 1979

Lions selection: George Fairbairn, Steve Evans, John Joyner, Mike Smith, Eric Hughes; John Holmes, Gary Stephens; George Nicholls captain, David Ward, Trevor Skerrett, Len Casey, Jeff Grayshon and Mick Adams. Subs: John Woods and Phil Hogan. *New Zealand selection*: James Leuluai [Auckland]; Dick Uluave [Manawatu], Olsen Filipaina [Auckland], Lewis Hudson [Canterbury], Dane O'Hara [Auckland]; Fred Ah Kuoi [Auckland], Gordon Smith [West Coast]; Mark Broadhurst [Canterbury], Howie Tamati [Taranaki], Dane Sorenson [Cronulla, Australia], Kevin Tamati [Wellington], Graham West [Taranaki, captain] and Tony Coll.Subs: David Smith [Auckland] and Paul Ravlich [Waikato]. Referee: Mr John Percival of Auckland.

Lions Versus New Zealand, Third Test, Carlaw Park, Aukland, 11 August 1979

Lions selection: George Fairbairn [Wigan]; Steve Evans [Featherstone Rovers], John Joyner [Castleford], Mike Smith [Hull Kingston Rovers], Eric Hughes [Widnes]; John Holmes [Leeds], Gary Stephens [Castleford]; George Nicholls [Widnes, captain], David Ward [Leeds], Trevor Skerrett [Wakefield Trinity], Len Casey [Bradford Northern], Jeff Grayshon [Bradford Northern] and Mick Adams [Widnes]. Subs: John Woods [Leigh] and Phil Hogan [Hull Kingston Rovers]. *New Zealand*: James Leuluai [Auckland]: Kevin Fisher [Waikato], Olsen Filiaino [Auckland], Lewis Hudson [Canterbury], Dane O'Hara [Auckland]; Fred Ah Kuoi [Auckland, captain], Shane Varley [Auckland]; Mark Broadhurst [Canterbury], Howie Tamati [Taranaki], Kevin Tamati [Wellington], Barry Edkins [Canterbury], Tony Coll [West Coast] and Mark Graham [Auckland]. Subs: David Smith [Auckland] and Paul Ravlich [Waikato].

CHAPTER 7

Yorkshire County Versus Cumbria, Derwent Park, Workington, 29 September 1979

Yorkshire team: Harold Box [Featherstone Rovers]; Andy Fletcher [Wakefield Trinity], Mick Parrish [Hunslet], Barry Banks [York], Steve Fenton [Castleford]; Steve Evans [Featherstone Rovers], Tony Dean [Hunslet]; Keith Tindall [Hull FC], Ronnie Wileman [Hull FC], Mick Gibbins, [Featherstone Rovers], Jeff Grayshon [Bradford Northern], Steve Hankins [Dewsbury] and Keith Bell [Featherstone Rovers]. Subs: Garry Smith [York] and Paul Norton [Castleford]. Cumbrian team: Steve Tickle [Barrow]; Ian MacCorquodale [Workington Town], Neil French [Barrow], Ian Ball [Barrow], Chris Camilleri [Barrow]; Ian Rudd [Workington Town], Arnie Walker [Workington Town]: Harold McCourt [Barrow], Alan Banks [Workington Town], Eddie Bowman [Leigh], Malcolm Flynn [Barrow], Les Gorley [Widnes] and David Hadley [Barrow]. Subs: Paul Charlton [Workington Town] and Bill Pattinson [Workington Town]. Referee: Mr Stan Wall of Leigh, attendance 3,427.

Bradford Northern Versus Widnes, John Player Trophy Final, Headingley, Leeds, 5 January 1980

Bradford Northern team: Keith Mumby; David Barends, David Redfearn, Derek

Parker, Les Gant; Nigel Stephenson, Alan Redfearn; Jimmy Thompson, Keith Bridges, Colin Forsyth, Jeff Grayshon, Gary Van Bellen and Len Casey. Subs: Steve Ferres and Ian Van Bellen. Widnes team: David Eckersley; Stuart Wright, Mal Aspey, Mick George, Mick Burke; Eric Hughs, Reg Bowden; Brian Hogan, Keith Elwell, Glynn Shaw, Les Gorley, David Hull and Mick Adams. Subs: John Myler and Jim Mills. Referee: Mr Billy Thompson of Huddersfield.

England Versus Wales, European Championship, Craven Park, Hull, 29 February 1980

England team: George Fairbairn [Wigan]; Stuart Wright [Widnes], John Joyner [Castleford], Mick Smith [Hull Kingston Rovers], Des Drummond [Leigh]; Steve Evans [Featherstone Rovers], Neil Holding [St Helens]; Roy Holdstock [Hull Kingston Rovers], David Ward [Leeds, captain], Keith Rayne [Wakefield Trinity], Len Casey [Hull Kingston Rovers], Peter Gorley [St Helens] and Harry Pinner [St Helens]. Subs: John Woods [Leigh] and Jeff Grayshon [Bradford Northern]. *Welsh team*: Harold Box [Featherstone Rovers]; Paul Prendiville [Hull FC], Graham Walters [Hull FC], Bill Francis [Oldham captain], Brian Juliff [Wakefield Trinity]; Paul Woods [Hull FC], Nes Flowers [Wigan]; Mel James [St Helens], Don Parry [Blackpool Borough], Glynn Shaw [Widnes], Chris Seldon [St Helens], John Bevan [Warrington] and Roy Mathias [St Helens]. Subs: Steve Dimond [Wakefield Trinity] and Mark McJennett [Barrow]. Referee: Mr Ron Campbell of Widnes, attendance 7,557.

England Versus France, European Championship, Narbonne, 16 March 1980

French team: F. Tranier; J.P. Rodriguez, J.M. Bourret, Christian Laumond, J.M. Gonzales; M. Mazare, Y. Greseque, Max Chantel, Henri Daniel, D. Hermet, Jose Gine, C. Baile and Joel Roosebrouck. Subs: J. Guige and M. Wermet. *English team:* George Fairbairn [Wigan]; Des Drummond [Leigh], John Joyner [Castleford], Mike Smith [Hull Kingston Rovers], Steve Evans [Featherstone Rovers]; John Woods [Leigh], Alan Redfearn [Bradford Northern]; Roy Holdstock [Hull Kingston Rovers], David Ward [Leeds, captain], Keith Rayne [Wakefield Trinity], Jeff Grayshon [Bradford Northern], Peter Smith [Featherstone Rovers] and Harry Pinner [Saints]. Subs: Peter Glynn [Saints] and Peter Gorley [Saints]. Referee: Mr Billy Thompson of Huddersfield, attendance 20,000.

Bradford Versus Widnes, Premiership Trophy Final, Station Road Swinton, 17 May 1980

Bradford Northern team: Mumby; MacLean, D. Redfearn, Parker, Gant, Stephenson, A. Redfearn, Thompson, Bridges, Forsyth, Clarkson, Grayshon, Hale. Subs: Ferres, G. van Bellen. *Widnes team*: Burke, Wright, George, Aspey, Bentley, Eckersley, Bowden, Shaw, Elwell, M. O'Neill, Gorley, Hull, Adams. Subs: Moran, Hogan. Referee: Mr Billy Thompson.

Yorkshire Versus Cumbria, County Championship, Craven Park, Hull, 17 September 1980

Yorkshire team: Geoff Wraith [Castleford]; Andy Fletcher [Wakefield Trinity], John Joyner [Castleford], Steve Quinn [Featherstone Rovers], Steve Fenton [Castleford];

Neil Hague [Leeds], Kevin Dick [Leeds]; Roy Holdstock [Hull Kingston Rovers], Bob Spurr [Castleford], Trevor Skerrett [Hull FC], Jeff Grayshon [Bradford Northern, captain], Kevin Rayne [Wakefield Trinity] and Steve Norton [Hull FC]. Subs: Steve Evans [Featherstone Rovers] and David Heron [Leeds], Yorkshire coach, Arthur Keegan. Cumbrian team: Steve Tickle [Barrow]; John Bulman [Whitehaven], Peter Stoddard [Whitehaven], Ian Ball [Barrow], Chris Camilleri [Barrow]; Ian Rudd [Workington Town], Arnold Walker [Whitehaven]; Eddie Bowman [Leigh], Alan McCurrie [Wakefield Trinity], John Cunningham [Workington Town], Vince Fox [Whitehaven], Les Gorley [Widnes] and Peter Gorley [St Helens]. Subs: Mel Mason [Barrow] and Malcolm Flynn [Barrow], Cumbrian coach Phil Kitchen. Referee: Mr Alec Givvons of Oldham, attendance was 3,400.

Lancashire Versus Yorkshire, County Championship, Naughton Park, Widnes, 24 September 1980

Yorkshire team: Geoff Wraith [Castleford]; Andy Fletcher [Wakefield Trinity], John Joyner [Castleford], Steve Quinn [Featherstone Rovers], Steve Fenton [Castleford]; David Topliss [Wakefield Trinity], Gary Stephens [Castleford]; Roy Holdstock [Hull Kingston Rovers], David Watkinson [Hull Kingston Rovers], Trevor Skerrett [Hull FC], Jeff Grayshon [Bradford Northern, captain], Kevin Rayne [Wakefield Trinity] and Steve Norton [Hull FC]. Subs: Tim Wilby [Hull FC] and David Heron [Leeds]. *Lancashire team*: Colin Whitfield [Salford], Keith Bentley [Widnes], Terry Bilsbury [Leigh], Martin Foy [Wigan], Jimmy Hornby [Wigan]; John Woods [Leigh], Neil Holding [St Helens]; Mike O'Neill [Widnes], Graham Liptrot [St Helens], Bob Eccles [Warrington], Steve O'Neill [Wigan], Alan Dearden [Widnes] and Mick Adams [Widnes]. Subs: Alan Fairhurst [Leigh] and Stan Gittins [Leigh]. Referee: Mr Ronnie Moore of Wakefield, attendance 2,000.

Great Britain Versus New Zealand, First Test, Central Park, Wigan, 18 October 1980

Great Britain team: George Fairbairn [Wigan, captain]; Chris Camilleri [Barrow], John Joyner [Castleford], Mike Smith [Hull Kingston Rovers], Keith Bentley [Widnes]; Steve Hartley [Hull Kingston Rovers], Kevin Dick [Leeds]; Roy Holdstock [Hull Kingston Rovers], David Watkinson [Hull Kingston Rovers], Trevor Skerrett [Hull FC], Jeff Grayshon [Bradford Northern], Les Gorley [Widnes] and Len Casey [Hull Kingston Rovers]. Subs: Mick Burke [Widnes] and Harry Pinner [St Helens]. New Zealand team: Mike O'Donnell [Canterbury]; Laurie Fisher [Waikato], James Leuluai [Auckland], Bruce Dickison [Canterbury], Dane O'Hara [Auckland]; Fred Ah Kuoi [Auckland], Gordon Smith [West Coast]; Mark Broadhurst [Canterbury], Alan Rushton [Canterbury], Kevin Tamati [Wellington], Tony Coll [West Coat], Graham West [Taranaki] and Mark Graham [North Sydney]. Subs: John Whittaker [Wellington] and Bob Baxendale [West Coast]. Referee: Mr Billy Thompson of Huddersfield, attendance 7,631.

Great Britain Versus New Zealand, Second Test, Odsal Stadium, Bradford, 2 November 1980

Great Britain team: George Faibairn [Wigan, captain]; Des Drummond [Leigh], John Joyner [Castleford], Mike Smith [Hull Kingston Rovers], Chris Camilleri

[Barrow]; Ken Kelly [Warrington], Kevin Dick [Leeds]; Roy Holdstock [Hull Kingston Rovers], Keith Elwell [Widnes], Glyn Shaw [Widnes], Jeff Grayshon [Bradford Northern], Len Casey [Hull Kingston Rovers] and Harry Pinner [St Helens]. Subs: Steve Evans [Featherstone Rovers] and Les Gorley [Widnes]. *New Zealand team*: Mike O'Donnell [Canterbury]; Gary Prohm [Auckland], John Whittaker [Wellington], James Leuluai [Auckland], Dane O'Hara [Auckland]; Fred Ah Kuoi [Auckland], Gordon Smith [West Coast]; Mark Broadhurst [Canterbury], Alan Rushton [Canterbury], Kevin Tamati [Wellington], Tony Coll [West Coast], Graham West [Taranaki] and Mark Graham [North Sydney, captain]. Subs: Laurie Fisher [Waikato] and Bob Baxendale [West Coast]. Referee: Mr Fred Lindop of Wakefield, attendance 11,000.

Great Britain Versus New Zealand, Third Test, Headingley, Leeds, 15 November 1980

Great Britain team: Mick Burke [Widnes]; Des Drummond [Leigh], John Joyner [Castleford], Steve Evans [Featherstone Rovers], John Atkinson [Leeds]; John Woods [Leigh], Arnie Walker [Whitehaven]; Trevor Skerrett [Hull], Keith Elwell [Widnes], Len Casey [Hull Kingston Rovers], Mick Adams [Widnes], Peter Gorley [St Helens], Steve Norton [Hull FC]. Subs: Ken Kelly [Warrington], Roy Holdstock [Hull Kingston Rovers]. *New Zealand team*: Mike O'Donnell [Canterbury]; Gary Prohm [Auckland], John Whittaker [Wellington], B.I. Dickison [Canterbury], Dane O'Hara [Auckland]; Fred Ah Kuoi [Auckland], Gordon Smith [West Coast]; Mark Broadhurst [Canterbury], Alan Rushton [Canterbury], Kevin Tamati [Wellington], B. Edkins [Canterbury], Graham West [Taranaki] and Mark Graham [North Sydney, captain]. Subs: Laurie Fisher [Waikato] and H. Tamati [Taranaki]. Referee W.H. Thompson of Huddersfield, attendance 8,210.

Yorkshire Versus Lancashire, County Championship, Wheldon Road, Castleford, 9 September 1981

Yorkshire team: Keith Mumby [Bradford Northern]; Terry Richardson [Castleford], John Joyner [Castleford], Les Dyl [Leeds], Steve Fenton [Castleford]; John Holmes [Leeds], Steve Nash [Salford]; Jeff Grayshon [Bradford Northern], David Ward [Leeds, captain], John Millington [Hull Kingston Rovers], Peter Smith [Featherstone Rovers], David Finch [Castleford] and Steve Norton [Hull FC]. Subs: Steve Quinn [Featherstone Rovers] and Brendon White [York]. *Lancashire team*: Colin Whitfield [Salford]; Des Drummond [Leigh], David Stephenson [Salford], Martin Foy [Wigan], Keith Bentley [Widnes]; Ken Kelly [Warrington]; Mike O'Neill [Widnes], Nicky Kiss [Wigan], Brian Case [Warrington], Ian Potter [Warrington], Mick Adams [Widnes] and Harry Pinner [St Helens]. Subs: Steve Donlan [Leigh] and Terry Flanagan [Oldham]. Referee: Mr Robin Whitfield of Widnes, attendance 1,222.

Bradford Versus Castleford, Yorkshire Cup Final, Headingley, Leeds, 3 October 1981

Castleford team: Claughton; Richardson, Fenton, Hyde, Morris; Joyner, Bob Beardmore; Hardy, Spurr, Barry Johnson, Finch, Kevin Ward and Timpson. Subs: Marchant and Norton. Bradford Northern team: Mumby; Barends, Hale, Alan Parker, Gant; Hanley, Alan Redfearn; Jeff Grayshon, Noble, Sanderson, Gary Van

Bellen, Graham Idle and Alan Rathbone. Subs: David Redfearn and Dick Jasiewicz.

Great Britain Versus France, First Test, The Boulevard, Hull, 6 December 1981

Great Britain team: George Fairbairn [Hull Kingston Rovers]; Des Drummond [Leigh], Mike Smith [Hull Kingston Rovers], John Woods [Leigh], Henderson Gill [Wigan]; Steve Hartley [Hull Kingston Rovers], Andy Gregory [Widnes]; Jeff Grayshon [Bradford Northern], David Ward [Leeds, captain], Trevor Skerrett [Hull FC], Les Gorley [Widnes], Peter Gorley [St Helens] and Steve Norton [Hull FC]. Subs: Mick Burke [Widnes] and Eddie Szymala [Barrow]. French team: Marcel Pillon [St Esteve]; Sebastian Rodriguez [Pia], Serges Costals [Villefranche], Hughes Ratier [Lezignan], Laurent Girardet [Pamiers]; Eric Waligunda [Lezignan], C. Scicchitano [Carpintras]; Henri Daniel [Pia], Christian Macalli [Villeneuve], Damian Verdieres [St Esteve], Jose Gine [Le Pont], Mark Ambert [Pia] and Joel Roosebrouck [Villeneuve]. Subs: Marcel Laville [Villeneuve] and Thierry Bernabe [Le Pont]. Referee: Greg Hartley of Australia, attendance 13,173.

France Versus Great Britain, Second Test, Stade Vélodrome, Marseilles, 20 December 1981

French team: Andre Perez [Toulouse]; Patrick Solal [Tonneins], Jacques Guigue [Avignon], Guy Delauney [Perpignan], Sebastian Rodriguez [Pia]; Michel Laville [Villeneuve], Christian Schicchitano [Carpentras]; Claude Zalduendo [Villeneuve], Jose Gine [Le Pontet], Guy Laforgue [Perpignan], Marc Ambert [Pia] and Joel Roosebrouck [Villeneuve, captain]. Subs: Etienne Kaminski [Albi] and Thierry Bernabe [Le Pontet]. *Great Britain team*: Mick Burke [Widnes]; Des Drummond [Leigh], Mike Smith [Hull Kingston Rovers], John Woods [Leigh], Henderson Gill [Wigan]; Steve Hartley [Hull Kingston Rovers], Andy Gregory [Widnes]; Jeff Grayshon [Bradford Northern], David Watkinson [Hull Kingston Rovers]. Trevor Skerrett [Hull FC], Les Gorley [Widnes], Eddie Szymala [Barrow] and Steve Norton [Hull FC]. Subs: George Fairbairn [Hull Kingston Rovers] and Peter Gorley [St Helens]. Referee: Greg Hartley of Australia, attendance 13,173.

Bradford Northern Versus Hull FC, Yorkshire Cup Final, Headingley, Leeds, 2 October 1982

Bradford team: Keith Mumby; David Barends, Les Gant, Alan Parker, Steve Pullen; Keith Whiteman, Dean Carroll; Jeff Grayshon, Brian Noble, Gary Van Bellen, Graham Idle, Dick Jasiewicz and Gary Hale. Subs: David Smith and Phil Sanderson. *Hull FC team*: Gary Kemble; Steve Evans, Terry Day, James Leuluai, Paul Prendiville; David Topliss, Kevin Harkin; Trevor Skerrett, Keith Bridges, Charlie Stone, Paul Rose, Lee Crooks and Mick Crane. Subs: Barry Banks and Steve Norton. Referee: Mr Stan Wall of Leigh, attendance 11,755.

CHAPTER 8

Australia Versus Great Britain, First Test, Boothferry Park, Hull, 30 October 1982

Great Britain team: George Fairbairn [Hull Kingston Rovers]; Des Drummond

[Leigh], Eric Hughes [Widnes], Les Dyl [Leeds], Steve Evans [Hull FC]; John Woods [Leigh], Steve Nash [Salford, captain]; Jeff Grayshon [Bradford Northern], David Ward [Leeds], Trevor Skerrett [Hull FC], Les Gorley [Widnes], Lee Crooks [Hull FC] and Steve Norton [Hull FC]. Subs: Ken Kelly [Warrington] and David Heron [Leeds]. *Australian team*: Greg Bretnall [Canterbury-Bankstown]; Kerry Boustead [Eastern Suburbs], Mal Meninga [South's, Brisbane], Steve Rogers [St George], Eric Grothe [Parramatta]; Brett Kenny [Parramatta], Peter Sterling [Parramatta]; Craig Young [St George], Max Krilich [Manly], Les Boyd [Manley], Wayne Pearce [Balmain], Rod Reddy [St George] and Ray Price [Parramatta]. Subs: Steve Ella [Parramatta] and John Muggleton [Parramatta]. Referee: Mon. J Rascagneres of France.

Australia Versus Great Britain, Second Test, Central Park, Wigan, 20 November 1982

Great Britain team: Keith Mumby [Bradford Northern]; Mike Smith [Hull Kingston Rovers], David Stephenson [Wigan], Henderson Gill [Wigan]; John Holmes [Leeds], Ken Kelly [Warrington]; Jeff Grayshon [Bradford Northern], John Dalgreen [Fulham], Trevor Skerrett [Hull FC], Bob Eccles [Warrington], Chris Burton [Hull Kingston Rovers] and David Heron [Leeds]. Subs: John Woods [Leigh] and Alan Rathbone [Bradford Northern]. *Australian team*: Greg Bretnall [Canterbury-Bankstown]; Kerry Boustead [Eastern Suburbs], Mal Meninga [South's, Brisbane], Steve Rogers [St George], Eric Grothe [Parramatta]; Brett Kenny [Parramatta], Peter Sterling [Parramatta]; Craig Young [St George], Max Krilich [Manly], Les Boyd [Manley], Wayne Pearce [Balmain], Rod Reddy [St George] and Ray Price [Parramatta]. Subs: Wally Lewis [Valley's, Brisbane] and Ray Brown [Manly]. Referee: Mon. J Rascagneres of France, attendance 23,216.

Great Britain Versus France, Limoux, 1 June 1985

Great Britain team: Shaun Edwards [Wigan];Joe Lydon [Widnes], David Creasser [Leeds], Keiron O'Loughlin [Widnes], Phil Ford [Wigan]; Ellery Hanley [Bradford Northern], Bob Beardmore [Castleford]; Jeff Grayshon [Bradford Northern], Nicky Kiss [Wigan], Neal Courtney [Wigan], David Heron [Leeds], John Fieldhouse [Widnes] and Ian Potter [Wigan]. Subs: Henderson Gill [Wigan], Mike Gregory [Warrington], Deryck Fox [Featherstone Rovers] and Roy Powell [Leeds]. *French team*: Serge Pallares [13 Catalan]; Hugues Ratier [Lezignan], Roger Palisses [Saint-Esteve], Philippe Fourquet [Toulouse], Didier Couston [Carpentras]; Luc Mendez [Limoux], Ivan Gresque [13 Catalan]; Max Chantal [Villeneuve], Thierry Bernabe [Le Pontet], Pierre Aillieres [Toulouse], Pierre Montgaillard [13 Catalan], Marc Palanque [Le Pontet] and Daniel Verdes [Villeneuve]. Subs: Serge Bret [Saint-Esteve], Francis Lope [Toulouse], Philippe Sokolow [Carcassonne], Patrick Alberola [Carcassonne], Jean-Louis Meurin [Albi] and Georges Alquier [Lezignan].

Great Britain Versus New Zealand, Second Test, Central Park, Wigan, 2 November 1985

Great Britain team: Mick Burke [Widnes]; Des Drummond [Leigh], Gary Schofield [Hull FC], Ellery Hanley [Wigan], Joe Lydon [Widnes]; Tony Myler [Widnes], Deryck Fox [Featherstone Rovers]; Jeff Grayshon [Leeds], David Watkinson [Hull Kingston

Rovers], John Fieldhouse [Widnes], Andy Goodway [Wigan], Ian Potter [Wigan] and Harry Pinner [St Helens]. Subs: Shaun Edwards [Wigan] and Chris Burton [Hull Kingston Rovers]. *New Zealand team*: Gary Kemble [Hull FC]; Dean Bell [Eastern Suburbs, Sydney], James Leuluai [Hull FC], Gary Prohm [Hull Kingston Rovers], Dane O'Hara [Hull FC]; Olsen Filipaina [Eastern Suburbs, Sydney captain], Clayton Friend [Auckland]; Kurt Sorenson [Cronulla, Sydney], Howie Tamati [Taranaki], Dane Sorenson [Cronulla, Sydney], Graham West [Wigan], Sam Stewart [Wellington] and Hugh McGahan [Eastern Suburbs, Sydney]. Subs: Fred Ah Kuoi [Hull FC] and Ricky Cowen [Aukland]. Referee: Mr Barry Gomersall of Queensland, attendance 16,000.

Great Britain Versus New Zealand, Third Test, Elland Road, Leeds, 9 November 1985

Great Britain team: Mick Burke [Widnes]; Des Drummond [Leigh], Gary Schofield [Hull FC], Shaun Edwards [Wigan], Joe Lydon [Widnes]; Ellery Hanley [Wigan], Deryck Fox [Featherstone Rovers]; Jeff Grayshon [Leeds], David Watkinson [Hull Kingston Rovers], John Fieldhouse [Widnes], Andy Goodway [Wigan], Ian Potter [Wigan] and Harry Pinner [St Helens]. Subs: Chris Arkwright [St Helens] and Lee Crooks [Hull]. *New Zealand team*: Gary Kemble; Darrell Williams [Auckland] Dean Bell, James Leuluai, Dane O'Hara; Fred Ah Kuoi. Clayton Friend; Kevin Tamati [Warrington], Wayne Wallace [Canterbury], Dane Sorenson, Mark Graham [North Sydney, captain] Kurt Sorenson and Gary Prohm, the subs were Olsen Filipaina and Hugh McGahan.

CHAPTER 9

Bradford Northern Versus Castleford, Yorkshire Cup Final, Headingley, Leeds, 17 October 1987

Castleford team: Rookley; Plange, Marchant, Beattie, Hyde; Joyner Southerwood; Shillito, Kevin Beardmore, Ward, Ketteridge, Fifita and Linder. Subs: Bob Beardmore and Sampson. Bradford team: Mercer; Ford, McGowan, Simpson, Francis; Mumby, Harkin; Jeff, Noble, Hill, Skerrett, Fairbank and Holmes. Subs: Roebuck and Hobbs. Referee: Mr Ken Allatt of Southport, attendance 11,000.

Featherstone Rovers Versus Bradford Northern, Yorkshire Cup Final, Headingley, Leeds, 5 November 1989

Bradford Northern team: Wilkinson; Cordle, McGowan, Simpson, Francis; Ivan Henjak, Harkin; Skerrett, Barraclough, Hamer, Hobbs, Fairbank and John Pendlebury. Subs: Mumby and Medley. Featherstone Rovers team: Bibb; Drummond, Ropati, Newlove, Banks; Smales, Fox; Grayshon, Trevor Clark, Bell, Gary Price, Booth and Peter Smith. Subs: Dakin and Fisher. Referee: Mr Robin Whitfield of Widnes, attendance 13,000.